Nederlandse Vereniging voor Rechtsvergelijking

opgericht op 20 januari 1968, statuten goedgekeurd bij K.B. van 28 juli 1969, no. 178

BESTUUR

prof. mr. H. J. M. Jeukens, voorzitter
prof. mr. H. U. Jessurun d'Oliveira, vice-voorzitter
mr. R. Kotting, sekretaris/penningmeester

prof. mr. B. Baardman, mr. H. Drion, prof. mr. W. Duk,
mr. D. C. Fokkema,prof. mr. Ch P. A. Geppaart, mr. A. G. Lubbers,
mr. S. K. Martens, prof. mr. J. G. Sauveplanne

Sekretariaat:

Oudezijds Achterburgwal 217-219, Amsterdam-1001, tel.: 020-5253403

Kontributie *f* 25,— per jaar (buitengewone leden waaronder studenten *f* 12,50) te voldoen door storting

op bankgiro AMRO 43.35.29.059

of postgiro 15.69.782 t.n.v. de penningmeester Ned. Ver. voor Rechtsvergelijking, Oudezijds Achterburgwal 217-219, Amsterdam

Losse exemplaren van de preadviezen verkrijgbaar bij de uitgever:
Kluwer B.V., Deventer, postbus 23, tel. (05700) 74411

DUTCH / ENGLISH COMPANY LAW

A comparative Review

by

Floris O. W. Vogelaar,

advocaat bij de Hoge Raad der Nederlanden

and

Martin G. Chester, LL.B.,

Solicitor of the Supreme Court

Springer-Science+Business Media, B.V.

ISBN 978-90-268-0719-0 ISBN 978-1-4899-6138-9 (eBook)
DOI 10.1007/978-1-4899-6138-9

Originally published by Kluwer Deventer in 1973

Index

List of Abbreviations

AGM	– Annual General Meeting
Art.	– Artikel (Article of the Commercial Code)
Artt.	– Artikelen
BV	– Besloten Vennootschap met Beperkte Aansprakelijkheid (Dutch 'private' company)
EEC	– European Economic Community
EGM	– Extraordinary General Meeting
GM	– General Meeting of Shareholders
G.m.b.H.	– Gesellschaft mit beschränkter Haftung (German 'private' company)
Hrgw.	– Handelsregisterwet (Trade Register Act)
K	– Wetboek van Koophandel (Dutch Commercial Code)
NV	– Naamloze Vennootschap (Dutch 'public' company)
PVBA	– Personen Vennootschap met Beperkte Aansprakelijkheid (Belgian 'private' company)
S.	– Section
SS.	– Sections
S.a.r.l.	– Société à responsabilité limitée (French 'private' company)
SER	– Sociaal Economische Raad (Dutch Social and Economic Council)
Stbl.	– Staatsblad (Dutch Government Gazette)
The 1948 Act	– The Companies Act, 1948
The 1967 Act	– The Companies Act, 1967
The Jenkins Report	– Report of the Company Law Committee (chaired by Lord Jenkins), as presented to Parliament by the President of the Board of Trade, June 1962 (Cmnd. 1749 of 1962)
The Prevention of Fraud Act	– The Prevention of Fraud (Investments) Act 1958
The Stock Transfer Act	– The Stock Transfer Act, 1963
The White Paper	– Company Law Reform (Cmnd. 5391 of 1973) as presented to Parliament by the Secretary of State for Trade and Industry, July 1973)
WJ	– Wet op de Jaarrekening van Ondernemingen (Dutch Annual Accounts Act)

Bibliography

The Netherlands:

1. Van der Grinten, W. C. L., Handboek voor de Naamloze Vennootschap (Tjeenk Willink, Zwolle, 1968).
2. Van der Grinten, W. C. L., Handboek voor de Naamloze en Besloten Vennootschap (Tjeenk Willink, Zwolle, 1971).
3. Jessurun d'Oliveira, H. U., De meerwaarde van rechterlijke uitspraken (Kluwer, Deventer, 1973).
4. Löwensteyn, F. J. W., De vennootschap met beperkte aansprakelijkheid (Kluwer, Deventer, 1970).
5. Lubbers, A. G./Scholten, Y., De Besloten Vennootschap (Tjeenk Willink, Zwolle, 1971).
6. Maeijer, J. M. M., Vennootschapsrecht in beweging (Samsom, Alphen a/d Rijn, 1971).
7. Van der Meer, S. W. Corporation Law of the Netherlands Antilles (Tjeenk Willink, Zwolle, 1973).
8. De Savornin Lohman, O., De S.E.R.-fusiecode en de beursoverval (Kluwer, Deventer, 1970).
9. Uniken Venema, C. Ae., Van Common Law en Civil Law. Inleiding tot het Anglo-Amerikaans recht in vergelijking met het Nederlandse (Tjeenk Willink, Zwolle, 1971).

England:

10. 'Admission of securities to listing', revised March 1973, published on the authority of The Stock Exchange – contains the detailed and technical regulations relating to the requirements for obtaining and maintaining listing on The Stock Exchange.
11. Campbell, A., The Industrial Relations Act – An Introduction (Longman, 1971).
12. 'The City-Code on Take-overs and Mergers' (with Practice Notes). Revised February 1972; published on the authority of the City Working Party.
13. Gower, L. C. B., Modern Company Law (3rd edition, Stevens) – a comprehensive treatment, less detailed but more analytical and theoretical than Palmer (see 14).
14. 'Palmer's Company Law', (+ 5th Cumulative Supplement, up-to-date to 1.1. 1973) 21st edition by Schmitthoff and Thompson, published by Stevens – a comprehensive practioner's book. It incorporates texts of the legislation.
15. Weinberg, M. A., Take-overs and mergers (3rd edition, Sweet & Maxwell) – comprehensive treatment of this subject, but it was published in 1971 and the Take-over Code has been revised since. It is therefore not up-to-date in that respect.

Introduction

We embarked upon the writing of this Review with the intention of revealing to its readers – within the restrictions we imposed upon ourselves because of the vast extent of the subject – the essential differences between the Company Laws of two Member States, in view of the move towards approximation of laws in the EEC. We feel that no approximation of laws can hope to gain acceptance unless it is based on a thorough understanding of the divergent rules which have to be reconciled, so as ultimately to have equivalent effect throughout all Member States. We have also made references, where appropriate, to the present draft EEC Directives on Company Law.

We also feel that the historical and present close commercial relationship between the two countries, based to no small extent upon similar attitudes to commerce, makes a comparison of an important part of their commercial laws the more interesting.

Finally, we feel that recent events, such as the revision of company legislation in Holland and the proposed revision in England, merger activity between Dutch and English companies, and growing interest in the Netherlands concerning the regulation of take-over activity whether international or internal, give such a study some topical importance.

From a stylistic point of view, we would liked to have written the Review as a single and integrated text. However, we decided that this would have involved a sacrifice of clarity and great over-use of the limited number of phrases which can be used to convey comparisons. We, therefore, decided upon the present form, which consists of dividing Company Law into a number of subjects and within each subject setting out firstly the position under Dutch law, secondly that under English law and thirdly drawing comparisons, when these appeared to us to be of interest and not necessarily self-evident.

We would also like to explain that the Review had to be written under some considerable pressure of time, due to the demands of everyday law practice. We, therefore, hope that our readers will appreciate three aspects; that we have, deliberately, omitted some aspects entirely, notably as to requirements relating to the public offering of securities, the law of agency, and liability of directors towards companies; that detail has sometimes been omitted for the sake of clarity of principle; and that there may be discovered some inaccuracies, or unjustified firmness of opinion on matters of uncertainty. Accordingly the Review should not be treated as being in any way an exhaustive treatment of Dutch or English Company Law or of the differences or similarities between them.

We have thought it advisable, for the sake of ease of reading, to omit any footnotes or marginal references. Instead we have provided a bibliography for those who may wish to look further into any aspects. We hope, nevertheless, that the Review will serve a useful purpose, as a guide both to those who wish to embark upon detailed comparative studies in this field and to the businessmen of either country whose interests are not confined to their own countries.

Terminology has caused us some problems, particularly in avoiding the use, when writing of Dutch law, of English words which are used by English lawyers to denote concepts familiar to them but which may not be at all the same as the Dutch legal concept for which, at first sight, the word appears an obvious translation. The best example which we can give of this is the word 'dissolution', which, as will become apparent in Chapter XI, under English law denotes the termination of the existence of a company *after* the liquidation process, whereas 'ontbinding' under Dutch law, although otherwise well translated by 'dissolution', denotes the process which *commences* liquidation and does not involve the termination at that stage of the company's juristic personality. The same difficulty is apparent in Article 5 (3) of the draft Second EEC Directive on Company Law which makes nonsense to a legal mind which is not acquainted with 'Continental' liquidation procedures.

Finally, we should both like to record our appreciation of the critical reading and constructive comments of Mr. Jan Maarten Boll as regards the Dutch law text and Mr. Michael Q. Walters as regards the English law text. We do not however, wish to attribute to them any responsibility for any possible lack of clarity or inaccuracy which still may occur in the final text of this Review.

London, September 1973

F. O. W. Vogelaar *M. G. Chester*

I. Sources of law; different types of companies

SOURCES OF LAW

Dutch law

101 Dutch Company law, which has always been mainly statutory law, has been subject to much discussion in the last two decades. It was felt that better forms of publicity for the company's business affairs–for the benefit of both shareholders and outsiders–had to be guaranteed. There also gradually grew a different attitude towards the definition of the basic aims of a company, once it had been created, resulting *inter alia* in the recognition of the necessity of workers' participation.

The developments in the field of harmonization of Company law in the former six EEC countries also contributed largely to the increasing need for a thorough revision of the law. One of the incentives to go ahead with such a revision at a somewhat quicker pace has been the adoption of the *First EEC Directive on Company Law* in 1968. All Member States had in their Company law a form of a private company or at least of a company which was meant to have few shareholders and–often–a rather limited scope of business (GmbH, Sarl, PVBA), whereas Dutch Company law had none.

In order to benefit fully from this First EEC Directive, a corresponding type of company was created in the form of the '*Besloten Vennootschap met beperkte aansprakelijkheid*' ('BV'), to form an alternative type of company to the already existing '*Naamloze Vennootschap*' ('NV').

102 The result of these developments was a thorough revision of Dutch Company law in 1970 and 1971 in which years no less than six major Acts became effective:

(a) Wet op de Jaarrekening van Ondernemingen (*Annual Accounts Act*), 10th September 1970, Stbl. (Government Gazette) 414, effective 1st May 1971;
(b) Herziening Enquêterecht (*Right of Inquiry Act*), 10th September 1970, Stbl. 411, effective 1st January 1971;
(c) Wet op de Ondernemingsraden (*Works Council Act*), 28th January 1971, Stbl. 54, effective 1st April 1971;
(d) Wet op de aanpassing aan de Eerste Richtlijn EEG (*Adaptation First EEC Directive Act*), 29th April 1971, Stbl. 285, effective 21st June 1971;
(e) Wet Besloten Vennootschap met Beperkte Aansprakelijkheid (*Private Company Act*), 3rd May 1971, Stbl. 286, effective 29th June 1971;
(f) Wet op de Structuren der NV en BV (*Structure of Public and Private Companies Act*), 6th May 1971, Stbl. 289, effective 1st July 1971.

103 Dutch Statutory Company law mainly forms a part of the Commercial Code (*'Wetboek van Koophandel'*) and apart from the Works Council Act and the Annual Accounts Act, the newly implemented Acts were all amalgamated with the Code's existing provisions, whereas the first two Acts mentioned remained Acts in their own right. Apart from the required revision of the Commercial Code, other statutory law had to be changed to cope with the overall revision. Major amendments were implemented in the *'Handelsregisterwet'* (Trade Register Act), which Act deals with all aspects of the filing in the Trade Register of companies' data, available for public inspection (free of charge).

104 It should, however, be noted that strong non-statutory sources of regulation of company also exist. These sources have a great effect on the practical application of Company law.

105 First of all should be mentioned the *Directives* issued by the *Ministry of Justice* from time to time, in which are set out the standards which the Ministry will apply as regards the wording and contents of the deeds of incorporation of all companies, when it comes to giving the Ministerial declaration of non-objection, required for the proper formation of a company or for the enactment of changes in its Articles of Association (*'Statuten'*). The Minister of Justice exercises his preventive supervisory powers relating to wording and contents of such deeds in accordance with the Directives prevailing at the time (see below in § 207).

106 In the second place the *'SER–Besluit Fusiegedragsregels 1971'* (*Dutch Take-over Code*) as laid down by the *'Sociaal Economische Raad'* (Social and Economic Council) may qualify as a non-statutory source of law. The Code's provisions should be observed in the event of mergers and take-overs and have a two-fold purpose: the protection of shareholders and the protection of employees. Although the Code has no statutory force, there is a sanction for non-observance consisting of a public announcement or rebuke by the *'Commissie voor Fusieaangelegenheden van de SER'* (Merger control Committee). If such a public rebuke is announced the result is that all members of the Stockbrokers Association (see § 107 below) cease to co-operate in the execution and completion of the take-over bid.

In this context it should be explained that the SER is a public body with mainly advisory powers in the area of industrial relations. Its tripartite composition includes employers, employees and neutral Government appointed representatives.

Further details of the Code in comparison with the City Code on Take-overs and Mergers are given in Chapter XII.

107 Thirdly the Stock Exchange Manual (*'Fondsenreglement'*) should be mentioned. Dutch companies which want to obtain listing on the Amsterdam Stock Exchange have to clear two hurdles. The Minister of Finance has to approve the listing under the Stock Exchange Act (*'Beurswet 1914'*) and the Board of the Amsterdam Stock Exchange, a private organisation organised by the Amsterdam Association of Stockbrokers (*'Vereeniging voor den Effectenhandel'*) also has to approve the listing.

The Stock Exchange Manual contains provisions concerning the requirements for obtaining and maintaining listing, and the Manual is drawn up by the Association's Board. It is also this Board which, by decision, varies the provisions of the Manual.

The Stock Exchange Manual contains detailed provisions relating to the 'prospectusses' of companies which want to obtain listing or which want to issue shares to the public. It also lays down minimum requirements for information which must be disclosed to the Board of the Association as well as minimum conditions for listing.

Although the Stock Exchange Manual is not statutory law, compliance with its rules is a pre-requisite of becoming or remaining listed.

108 Last but not least, case law qualifies as a source of non-statutory Company law. Although the Netherlands do not have a system of binding precedent, in practice the Dutch Courts constantly develop and refine by interpretation the standards of Company law, in particular where take-over bids, minority shareholdings or workers' participation are concerned.

English law

109 The legal systems of England and Wales on the one hand and Scotland on the other hand are separate and in very many aspects completely different in substance – Scottish law having its origins in Roman law to a much greater extent than English law. It is conventional to refer to the law of England and Wales collectively as 'English law' as the same law applies in both areas.

Although it is, therefore, not meaningful to speak of 'British law', Company law is one of the parts of law in Britain which has been the subject of extensive legislation and, apart from a few differences which are largely due to the different nature of English and Scottish property law, the companies' legislation applies equally to England (including Wales) and Scotland. This review however deals with Company law as it applies in England and Wales. The Company law of Northern Ireland, although in many respects similar to that of England, is a completely separate system with separate legislation as, indeed, is that of the Republic of Ireland.

The present consolidation of Company law is contained in the *Companies Act 1948* ('the 1948 Act') the latest of a series of Acts stretching back to the beginning of the present century. It is not a codification in the strict sense as large areas of Company law are not covered by it but remain as 'common law', dependent on judicially decided cases.

110 It may be useful at this point to explain that, under the English legal doctrine of 'binding precedent', Judges are, with some exception, bound to follow previous decisions of Judges of Superior Courts on the same principle of law. As a result a large part of English law including, as mentioned, Company law, consists of the principles determined in decided cases before the Courts, sometimes followed and developed over a long period of time. Until quite recently a wrong decision on a matter of law could only be overruled either by a Superior Court or by legislation. Judges however often found, and continue to find, it possible to 'distinguish' the principle in a previously decided case from that in the case before them. In this way they avoid having to apply the principle where they consider it inappropriate. In the last few years the highest English Court of law, the House of Lords, has decided that it is no longer bound to follow its own previous decisions and this has considerably eased the difficulty created by the fact that previously incorrect or obsolete principles decided upon by the House of Lords could only be reversed by legislation.

111 Since the enactment of the 1948 Act, an official committee has considered further reform of Company law and in 1962 it published a report recommending many changes of substance and detail ('The Jenkins Report'). There was a new Companies Act in 1967 but this only partially implemented these recommendations and was not a consolidating Act. The 1948 and the 1967 Acts therefore have to be considered together and are commonly referred to as 'the Companies Acts 1948 to 1967', or merely as '*the Companies Acts*'.

The remainder of the recommendation in the Jenkins Report remain to be implemented and due to pressure on the Parliamentary timetable it is only in this year, 1973, that the Government has put forward proposals for the implementation, with some modifications, of the rest of the recommendations together with some important new proposals for other reforms of Company law. A consultative document of rather general scope ('*the White Paper*') was issued by the Government in July 1973 and it is proposed that a Companies Bill should be published later this year for enactment, it is hoped, not later than next year.

112 In consequence of the United Kingdom's accession to the EEC, some amendments to Company law were made in the *European Communities Act, 1972,* principally to modify the ultra vires doctrine in favour of a person dealing with a company in good faith, to make personally liable those who act in the name or on behalf of a company before it is formed and to make changes in the system of official filing of certain information and documents relating to companies.

113 In addition to the Companies Acts there are other statutes on closely-related topics, such as the *Prevention of Fraud (Investments) Act, 1958* (regulating attempts to induce members of the public to purchase or dispose of securities, take-over bids, brokers and dealers in securities, and other matters), the *Stock Transfer Act, 1963* (simplifying requirements for instruments of transfer of shares and other securities) and the *Protection of Depositors Act, 1963* (regulating advertisements for the deposit of money).

114 In addition to Company law, there are other ways in which the conduct of companies and their officers is regulated. Though not having the force of law, they do have considerable influence upon corporate and financial practice:

The City Code on Take-overs and Mergers

115 In 1967 various bodies in the City of London set up a Working Party on Take-overs and Mergers following public disquiet about practices during such transactions. The Working Party published the above-mentioned Code consisting of general principles followed by more detailed Rules for the conduct of take-over bids. The Code has since been revised and amplified. As in the case of The Stock Exchange regulations, the Code does not have the force of law but failure to observe it can result not only in disapproval but in the application of more effective sanctions such as suspension of listing of a company's securities. The last sanction is a two-edged weapon, since suspension deprives all a company's shareholders of the market for their securities. The Code is administered by the Panel on Take-overs and Mergers and further consideration will be given to it in Chapter XII below.

Stock Exchange Regulations

116 In 1973 The Stock Exchange, London, and all the provincial stock exchanges in England, Wales, Scotland and Ireland were united into a single Exchange with common regulations, although separate trading floors still exist in the various commercial centres of these countries. A company desiring to obtain or maintain listing of its securities must comply with the regulations of The Stock Exchange which thereby exerts considerable influence and control over the conduct of such companies. The regulations only apply to listed companies. The regulations cover not only the requirements for obtaining listing but also such matters as mergers, acquisitions, and realizations, disclosure of interests and, possibly most importantly, presentation of accounts.

Historically, Stock Exchange requirements, particularly as to accounts, have been, and still remain, in advance of companies' legislation in the United Kingdom.

The Stock Exchange Regulations do not have the force of law as such. However, there is a procedure provided in S. 39 of the 1948 Act under which in suitable cases compliance with the detailed prospectus requirements of the Act can be dispensed with if the Stock Exchange grants a certificate of exemption (to the extent specified in the certificate of exemption) and provided that the Stock Exchange Regulations are complied with. The regulations in such a case are therefore indirectly given the force of law. Furthermore the fact that listing cannot be obtained without complying with the Regulations and that it may be suspended or withdrawn if the regulations are broken, constitutes an extra-legal sanction whose effectiveness, however, depends upon the circumstances.

Accountancy requirements

117 The Companies Acts lay down minimum requirements for company's accounts. As mentioned above, The Stock Exchange imposes more stringent requirements in the case of listed companies. In addition to this, the professional accountancy bodies in the United Kingdom most concerned with the auditing of corporate accounts have over the last few years carried out a considerable amount of research into various aspects of accounting practice. They have published several 'statements of standard accounting practice' and more are proposed.

It is intended that accountants in certifying the accounts of companies should require that they be presented in accordance with the standard statements. As an auditor's certificate is a necessary part of a company's accounts, these standard statements may be expected to be followed and should result in fuller disclosure and uniformity of presentation. These statements apply particularly to listed companies but in some cases also to unlisted ones.

Comparison

118 Dutch case law is confined to refinement and interpretation of the general principles of law such as that of 'good faith' (e.g. in relationship between shareholders) as all major areas of Company law are dealt with in considerable detail in statutes. English case law on the other hand also has to cover some major areas not dealt with by statutes, e.g. the rules as to payment of dividends out of profits and not out of capital (see §§ 807–810 below) and the extent to which companies are bound by unauthorised acts of its representatives. This latter topic is considered too large and technical for this review but is mentioned again in connection with management in Chapter V.

DIFFERENT TYPES OF COMPANIES

Dutch law

119 For the purposes of this comparative review consideration is confined to the two types of companies limited by shares, the Naamloze Vennootschap (NV) and the Besloten Vennootschap met Beperkte Aansprakelijkheid (BV), as defined in Artt. 36 and 57 K.

In principle the NV and the BV are very similar in nature and structure. The Articles of Association may even be identical. However, a BV has–as does the English private company–to impose certain restrictions in its Articles of Association. Whereas shareholders in a NV, in principle, are free to transfer their shares, the BV-shareholder may do so freely only to relatives, but even in such a case the Articles of Association may restrict or exclude such transfer. All other transfer of BV-shares must either be subject to the approval of the General Meeting of Shareholders ('GM') or the transferor must offer the shares to be transferred to the other shareholders first, before being free to transfer to outside transferees.

Furthermore, as distinct from the NV (which may by its Articles of Association provide for both, or either type of shares), the BV can have no bearer shares, but only registered shares. It may not issue share certificates (Art. 57 K). The BV must maintain a share register and may issue to a shareholder an extract from that register in respect of his shares (Art. 57k K) on request.

Finally, a different treatment exists between the NV and the BV as regards the publication of annual accounts. This is dealt with below in §§ 830–832.

It must be clear from both the Articles of Association and from the name of the company, what type of company is used. The company's name must bear 'NV' or 'BV' before or after its name, and BV Articles of Association have to incorporate the restrictions mentioned above.

English law

120 Although by far the majority of companies are formed by incorporation under the Companies Acts this is not the only possible method. In addition to such companies, commonly referred to as 'registered companies', there are companies formed for special purposes under general Acts of Parliament or special Acts of Parliament, companies formed under Royal Charter, and costbook companies (a hybrid form of corporation and partnership).

121 There are also several types of registered company, for example companies limited by guarantee, whether with or without a share capital. However, by far the most common type of company is that limited by shares. The rest of this Review so far as English law is concerned will be confined to the registered company limited by shares. The basic principle is that the members' liability to contribute towards the company's debts is limited to the nominal amount of the shares which they have subscribed. Once these shares have been 'paid up', the members have no further liability. Companies limited by shares must take one of two forms; either a private company or a public company.

122 The basic distinction between these two types of company is that a company can only be private if (S. 28. 1948 Act):

(a) there is a restriction on the right of the members to transfer their shares;
(b) there is a limitation on the number of members to fifty. However this need not include employees who hold shares and former employees who were shareholders when employed and who continue to hold their shares after the end of their employment; and
(c) any invitation to the public to subscribe for shares or debentures is prohibited.

There is therefore a presumption, which can be rebutted, that a company is a public company. This is rebutted by the existence in its constitution of the above restrictions.

123 The restriction on transfer of shares can take several forms, such as the Board of Directors having a discretion to decline to register a transfer to any person of whom they do not approve or an obligation to offer shares to the other shareholders before being free to transfer to non-shareholders. Exceptions are sometimes permitted for transfers to relatives but this is not obligatory.

There is no legal objection to the Articles of Association of a public company containing some form of restriction on the transfer of shares, although this will cause difficulty if listing is sought on The Stock Exchange.

124 The difference in the application of the Companies Acts to public and private companies may be summarised by stating that the following provisions apply only to public companies:

(i) the minimum number of members is seven (private company: two)–S. 1. 1948 Act;
(ii) on incorporation a public company may not commence business until it has obtained a 'trading certificate'. To obtain this a prospectus must either be issued or a 'statement in lieu of prospectus' must be filed (S. 109. 1948 Act). (See further in § 227 below);
(iii) a statutory meeting must be held and the directors must make a statutory report to the members (S. 130. 1948 Act). This meeting has to be held shortly after the company becomes entitled to commence business;
(iv) a public company must, unless registered before November 1st, 1929, have at least two directors (S. 176. 1948 Act);
(v) there must be filed with the Registrar of Companies written consents of the directors where it is intended that directors should be appointed in the Articles (S. 181. 1948 Act);
(vi) apart from the first directors, subsequent directors must be elected by separate resolutions in general meeting unless a unanimous resolution has first been passed that two or more may be appointed by a single resolution (S. 183. 1948 Act);
(vii) it follows from the fact that transfer of shares of a private company must be restricted, that only a public company can issue bearer shares. However, this is of little practical importance for exchange control reasons explained in § 303 below;
(viii) there is an age limit for retirement of directors of public companies (S. 185. 1948 Act and see further in § 528 below);
(ix) a person attending a general meeting of a public company as proxy for a shareholder is not entitled to speak but only to vote unless the Articles of Association permit him to speak as well. In the case of a private company he may speak and vote regardless of any provisions of the Articles of Association (S. 136. 1948 Act).

125 Unless otherwise authorised by the Department of Trade & Industry, both public and private companies must incorporate the word 'Limited' in their names (S. 2. 1948 Act). There is, however, no present requirement to specify in the name whether the company is public or private, nor need this expressly be stated in the company's constitution, it being sufficient that the restrictions mentioned above are contained in it. One of the proposals in the White Paper is that the fact that a company is a private one should be made explicit in its title.

126 Private companies are typically used for small or family businesses and as subsidiaries of public companies. Most public companies are originally formed as private companies and only converted to public companies prior to and for the purpose of obtaining listing on The Stock Exchange.

In the White Paper the Government reveals that it proposes to re-define the status of a private company and also to define explicitly the term 'public company'. These proposals are dealt with further in § 313 below.

Comparison

127 Although the law applicable to the various types of company has yet to be dealt with in detail in this review, some differences have already become apparent, especially between BV's and private companies which might at first sight appear to be the same in view of their common place and function in commercial life.

The private company has different rules from the BV in respect of:

(i) *The name:* One cannot tell from the name that the company is private;
(ii) *Number of members:* The restriction, in general, to 50. The exception for employees and ex-employees removes one potential barrier to the holding by employees of shares in the company for which they work;
(iii) *Issue of debentures to the public;*
(iv) *Accounts:* Private companies are subject to the same basic accounting requirements as public companies.

'LARGE COMPANIES'

Dutch law

128 Apart from the distinction between the NV and BV type of company, yet another demarcation line between different types of companies may be drawn. This division is making a distinction between 'normal' and 'large' companies and equally applicable to BV's and NV's (Art. 58c K).

The Commercial Code contains a number of general provisions solely relating to companies above a certain size. The cumulative criteria for such a company are:

(i) it has an issued capital and reserves totalling at least Dfl. 10,000,000;
(ii) it, or a legal entity in which it participates beneficially to the extent of at least 50%, has pursuant to a legal obligation to do so (see Artt. 2 and 3 Works Council Act) formed a Works Council; and
(iii) it and a legal entity in which it participates beneficially to the extent of at least 50%, together employ, as a rule, at least 100 persons in the Netherlands (Art. 52c K).

If and so long as a company meets these conditions, it is under an obligation to register a statement in the Trade Register, indicating that the company meets the size requirements. After a period of three years in which a company continuously remains registered for these purposes, it has to comply with a special management regime, which applies by virtue of the 'Structure of Public and Private Companies Act' – the so-called 'Structure-Provisions'. This obligation ends three years after the entry of such a statement in the Trade Register is no longer required and has been withdrawn (Art. 52d K).

129 The structure provisions basically provide for a compulsory two-tier management system. A supervisory *Board of 'Commissarissen'* (*'Raad van Commissarissen'*) of at least three persons has to be established, supervising the board of directors' activities. For details, however, see below in §§ 517–523.

Two major exceptions to the obligatory implementation of the structure provisions should be mentioned:

130 In the first place the following 'large' companies need not be registered as such and are therefore completely exempted (Art. 52c (3) K):

(i) a company beneficially owned to the extent of at least 50% by one or more other 'large' companies; or
(ii) a 'pure' holding and financing company, provided the majority of the employees of the companies in its group are employed outside the Netherlands; or
(iii) a company rendering administrative and financial services to companies referred to under (ii) above and to affiliated Dutch companies.

131 The second exemption is only partial insofar as it permits the Articles of Association to provide that the GM instead of the board of 'Commissarissen' appoints and dismisses directors and/or adopts the annual accounts. This, however, only applies in the case of those 'large' companies which are beneficially owned to the extent of at least 50%:

(a) by a legal entity, the majority of whose employees are employed outside the Netherlands; or
(b) under a joint-venture agreement, by two or more legal entities as referred to under (a); or
(c) under a joint venture agreement, by one or more legal entities referred to under (a) and one or more 'large' companies.

132 Furthermore the above partial exception is not applicable if the majority of the combined number of employees of the company in question and the legal entity/entities referred to under (a), (b) or (c) is employed within the Netherlands. In other words, only those companies which have their 'centre of gravity' outside the Netherlands may opt for the partial or 'mitigated' structure regime (Art. 52e K).

133 A final exemption is to be found in Art. 52f K, where the Minister of Justice, after consultation with the SER, may declare one or more of the structure provisions

(Artt. 52h–n K) inapplicable. Such exemption may be conditional and can be withdrawn at any time.

English law and Comparison

134 Special provisions, which are outside the scope of this review, apply to insurance and banking companies, particularly as to accounts and reserves. There are, however, no obligations which apply to the British companies solely by reason of size of capital or number of employees. In particular there is no provision in British companies' legislation for the appointment of any supervisory board of directors, a single board of directors being the rule. However, there is no prohibition against giving certain directors specified supervisory functions, as set out further in §§ 524–525 below.

135 In addition to complying with the regulations of The Stock Exchange, when any shares or debentures of a public company are listed, further provisions of the Companies Acts apply as follows:

(i) the company must maintain a register showing any interest of one-tenth or more of any class of the share capital which does not have restricted voting rights. There is a corresponding obligation imposed upon the holders of such an interest to notify the company (SS. 33–4. 1967 Act);
(ii) directors of the company or of associated companies may not deal in options to buy or sell any listed shares or debentures of the company (S. 25. 1967 Act).

Whether or not any shares or debentures are listed, the auditor of any company which has offered shares or debentures to the public must either be a member of a recognised body of accountants or be otherwise recognised by the Department of Trade & Industry as qualified (S. 16.1948 Act and S. 13.1967 Act).

LEGAL ENTITY

Dutch law

136 All NV and BV companies are legal entities in their own right (Artt. 37 and 57 K). This legal status becomes effective as from the company's formation provided that the Ministerial declaration of non-objection has been obtained. Directors, however, remain jointly and severally liable to third parties for all acts performed by them before registration of the company's business at the Trade Register and before at least 10% of the par value of each share, issued upon the formation, has been paid up (Art. 36g K), notwithstanding that the company also becomes liable.

137 Artt. 40 and 57r K open up the possibility of performing acts on behalf of a company which is in the process of formation. These may result in binding contracts for the company if after incorporation it confirms such acts either expressly or tacitly. If the company does not confirm the act, those who performed it are liable jointly and severally for the damages suffered by the third party as a consequence thereof unless otherwise stipulated.

English law

138 All registered companies are legal entities in their own rights and this status becomes effective from the date of incorporation mentioned in the Certificate of Incorporation (S. 13. 1948 Act and see further in § 209 below). From that date the company is capable of exercising all the functions of an incorporated company, subject only in the case of a public company to the restrictions on commencement of business referred to in § 227 below.

139 Unless otherwise agreed, where a contract purports to be made by a company or by a person as agent for a company at a time when the company has not come into existence, then it takes effect as a contract entered into by the person purporting so to act and he is personally liable accordingly (European Communities Act–S. 9 (2)). The company itself cannot enforce the contract or have the contract enforced against it, even after incorporation.

Comparison

140 A significant difference here is in the enforcement of contracts entered into before the company comes into existence.

II. Formation of a Company

FORMATION DOCUMENTS

Dutch law

201 In order to form a company under Dutch law, specific consensus of the prospective incorporators is required on the name, domicile, object, capital structure and on appointment of the first managing director(s) of the company.

This consensus is contained in only one instrument–the notarial deed of incorporation–in which the company's Articles of Association are also set out.

English law

202 The document required for the constitution of a registered company, whether public or private, is under English law divided into two parts, the first being called the Memorandum of Association and the second the Articles of Association. The Memorandum of Association is intended to contain the fundamental law of the company and there are restrictions on alteration of certain of its provisions. The Articles of Association on the other hand are freely alterable by the GM.

Memorandum of Association

203 This must be in accordance with a form set out in Table B in the First Schedule to the 1948 Act or as near thereto as circumstances admit. It must therefore contain at least the following (S. 11. 1948 Act):

1. Name Clause
2. Registered Office clause
3. Objects clause
4. Limited liability clause
5. Capital clause
6. Clause by which the incorporators agree to form the company

Articles of Association

204 These contain the regulations as between the shareholders, for the management and conduct of the business of the company. There is set out as Table A in the First Schedule to the 1948 Act ('Table A') a specimen form of regulations and these apply in all cases in which they are not excluded or modified by Articles registered with the Registrar. Accordingly it is not necessary to register any Articles of Association at all but it is normal to do so in order to have regulations exactly suited to the wishes of the prospective shareholders. There are, therefore, three possibilities:

(i) no articles are registered: Table A applies without modification;
(ii) complete articles are registered and the whole of Table A is excluded. This is common in the case of public companies listed on The Stock Exchange;
(iii) articles are registered modifying or excluding only part of Table A. Table A then applies as modified and together with any supplementary regulations set out in the registered articles. This is common in the case of private companies.

Comparison
205 Self-evident.

FORMATION PROCEDURE

Dutch law
206 The actual formation takes place by notarial deed of incorporation, containing the company's Articles of Association, the names of the two or more incorporators (they or their proxies sign the deed together with the notary public), a statement of the required capital subscriptions and the appointment of the first director(s) (Artt. 36b, c and d; and 57a, b and c K). The notarial deed must be in the Dutch language.

207 As already stated above the formation of a company is subject to the '*declaration of non-objection*' by the Minister of Justice (Artt. 36 and 57 K). Such declaration may only be refused for the reason that–in view of the intentions or the antecedents of those who will define or help define the company's policy (i.e. the incorporators)– a serious danger exists that the company will be used for unlawful purposes, or that its activities will be pursued to the detriment of creditors; that the Articles of Association are contrary to morality, public order or law, or that, it is not shown that the incorporators will take up at least one fifth of the company's authorised share capital (Artt. 36e and 57c K).

The Ministry for these purposes examines the draft deed of incorporation and the credentials of the incorporators, the first director(s) and the first members of the board of 'Commissarissen' (if any). The Directives give further details as to what criteria the Minister will use in approving of the incorporators, first directors or 'Commissarissen'.

English law
208 The incorporators must sign both the Memorandum of Association and the Articles of Association in the presence of a witness, who does not have to have any official qualification. In the case of a private company there must be at least two incorporators; in the case of a public company at least seven. The compulsory provisions of the Memorandum are referred to above. (There does not appear to be any legal rule as to whether the Memorandum and Articles may be in a foreign language but it is thought that in practice the Registrar would not accept it.) In the Memorandum and Articles the incorporators each agree to take a specified number of

shares, which can be as little as one each. The shares can be of any nominal value agreed upon by them.

The first directors of the company can be nominated in the Articles of Association but are frequently only appointed after incorporation.

209 The application for registration is made to the Registrar of Companies and must consist of the following:

1. Memorandum and Articles of Association duly signed and stamped.
2. A Statutory Declaration of compliance with the formation requirements. This has to be made before a Commissioner for Oaths and must be signed either by a solicitor engaged in the formation or by a person named in the Articles as a director or secretary of the company.
3. In the case of a public company there must also be lodged the consent in writing of every person at the time prepared to act as a director together with a list of those who have consented to act as directors.

After payment of the registration fee (see § 245 below) and official examination by the office of the Registrar, a Certificate of Incorporation will be issued. The Registrar may decline to register a company if any of its objects are illegal, but apart from this does not in practice exert any control over the contents of the Memorandum and Articles of Association provided that they contain the provisions required by law (S. 1(1). 1948 Act).

The Certificate of Incorporation is conclusive evidence that all the requirements of the Act in respect of registration have been complied with and that the association is a company authorised to be registered and duly registered (S. 15(1). 1948 Act).

If the Registrar declines to register a company in compliance with the Act, the Court may examine the matter and if it thinks fit order him to register it.

Comparison

210 There is no comparable requirement under English law to the Dutch declaration of non-objection, the function of the Registrar of Companies under English law in connection with company formation being essentially that of registration rather than supervision.

SHAREHOLDERS/MEMBERS

Dutch law

211 In Artt. 36a and 57c K it is stated that the fact that one or more persons cease to participate in the company does not affect the validity of the participation of the remaining members. In other words, although for the formation of a company two or more incorporators have to participate, a company–once in existence–may have only one shareholder. This rules out the necessity of having nominee shareholdings.

There are no legal limits as to the number of shareholders in the various types of companies as long as the requirement of plurality in the incorporation phase is met. An NV therefore may end up with only one shareholder (e.g. a 100% subsidiary), whereas a BV may have as many shareholders as desired, or vice-versa.

English law

212 If the number of members falls below the requirements of the 1948 Act, the company nevertheless continues to exist although this is a ground on which the Court may order it to be wound-up. This is so even if eventually there are no directors or shareholders alive. In such a case a procedure provided by S. 131 and 135 of the 1948 Act may resolve the problem as these sections empower one member to apply to the Department of Trade & Industry for a GM to be held and the Court to order a GM to be called if it is impracticable to call it in the manner prescribed by the Articles or the Act. If the number of shareholders falls below the legal minimum and the company continues to carry on business for more than six months, each member who is aware of the position becomes severally liable for all debts contracted by the company after such six months' period. This is an exception to the rule of limited liability and is in addition to the company's liability.

As mentioned above, the maximum number of members of a private company is restricted. There is no such restriction in the case of a public company.

Comparison

213 It is noteworthy that the provision of Art. 5 (2) of the draft Second EEC Directive that at least six months must be allowed for the regularisation of a deficiency of numbers before winding-up is ordered is not at present complied with under English law. It would in any event be inapplicable under Dutch law as a deficiency of numbers is not a ground for winding-up.

NAME

Dutch law

214 A company's name must have a certain measure of distinction, and may not resemble too closely an already existing name of a company engaging in similar activities, nor may it be misleading in any other way. Subsidiaries may bear a name containing elements of a foreign parent company's name, except that a reference to the parent company's legal status may not be included.

In order to avoid misleading or confusing names the Ministry of Justice demands that prior to the formation of the company the proposed name should be cleared with all Chambers of Commerce in the Netherlands, these Chambers being the places where the Trade Registers are kept.

English law

215 Because of the large number of registered companies and the consequent possibility of similarity in name, it is the normal practice to obtain provisional approval from the Department of Trade & Industry through the Registrar of Companies in advance of incorporation. This is because the Department of Trade & Industry may refuse the registration of a name which in its opinion is undesirable. The Department also has power to compel an existing company to change its name within six months after registration if it is too similar to that of an existing registered company or at any time if the name is so misleading as to be likely to cause harm to the public. The Department from time to time issues Practice Notes as a guide to the way in which its discretion over names is exercised. These Notes, however, have no statutory effect.

Comparison

216 The Practice Notes of the English Department of Trade & Industry to some extent cover one of the purposes of the Dutch Ministerial Directives.

OBJECT

Dutch law

217 Generally a company may enter into any type of legitimate business. The objects of the company must be stated in the Articles of Association and should indicate the nature of the company's business.

It is typical of Dutch objects clauses that these are agreeably short and expressed in a very wide sense. The company's main activities should feature in the text, whereas all activities related to the main object are usually covered in a sentence like '... and furthermore to perform all those activities required in the widest sense for the promotion of this object, participation in other companies not excluded'.

218 As a result of the First EEC Directive, Artt. 36h and 57c K provide that no company can plead that an act performed in its name was ultra vires, unless it can prove that the other party knew that this was the case, or that the other party could not reasonably have been ignorant of this fact. The other party, however, has no right to invoke the 'ultra vires' doctrine as regards his obligations towards the company. Yet another result of the EEC rules is to be found in Artt. 36i and 57c K, where it is laid down that if the notarial deed of incorporation has been made up in accordance with all the requirements and, furthermore, the declaration of non-objection is obtained, defects in the instrument of incorporation do not affect the validity of the company.

English law

219 As stated above, one of the compulsory provisions in the Memorandum of Association is the 'objects clause' which states the purpose for which the company is incorporated. This clause is normally of a very lengthy and detailed nature in order to reduce as far as possible the risk of the company doing something for which it lacks power, and also because English Courts in construing such a provision apply the '*eiusdem generis*' rule so that provisions of a general nature are treated as relating to and being restricted by those of a more specific nature.

220 Until the passing of the European Communities Act, if a company entered into a contract which was outside its powers *('ultra vires')* neither the company nor the other party to the contract could bring legal proceedings to enforce it. The company's powers are those set out in its objects clause. S. 9 (1) of the European Communities Act is supposed to implement the First EEC Directive in that respect and restricts the application of the ultra vires doctrine though not abolishing it. The doctrine can no longer be relied upon by the company against the other party if both of the following conditions were satisfied:

(i) the other party to the contract acted in good faith. The problem here is that 'good faith', although an expression used in many branches of English law, is not defined for the purposes of the Act and there is therefore an area of doubt whether the third party acts in good faith if he is merely deemed to have notice that the transaction is ultra vires as opposed actually to having notice of that fact.
   Again before the passing of the European Communities Act, a person dealing with a company was deemed to have notice of anything contained in its registered documents and therefore of the extent of its powers under its Memorandum of Association. However, S. 9 (1) also provides that the power of the directors to bind the company is deemed free of any limitation under the Memorandum or Articles of Association and it therefore now seems that unless the other party actually knew that the company did not have power to enter into the contract, the 'ultra vires' doctrine could not be invoked against him.
(ii) The transaction in question has been decided on by the directors.

However, it seems that the other party can still invoke the 'ultra vires' doctrine against the company and the doctrine continues to apply as between the directors and the shareholders or the directors and the company.

Comparison

221 It might be thought that the provisions of S. 9(2) of the European Communities Act would result in a shortening of the present lengthy provision of English objects clauses to something more resembling the Dutch pattern. However this does not seem likely since firstly there remains the problem of the third party who has notice of the provisions of the objects clause and does not therefore enjoy the 'good faith' protection and secondly one of the reasons for such length is the English Courts' approach to construction of documents referred to above.

DOMICILE AND RESIDENCE

Dutch law
222 The company's registered office should be in the Netherlands (Artt. 36c and 57b K). The actual centre of activity, however, may be situated elsewhere, if that is thought to be more convenient for the pursuance of its objects.

English law
223 The situation of the registered office determines also the *domicile* of the English company although not its residence. The country of situation of the registered office must be stated in the company's Memorandum of Association i.e. whether England (including Wales) or Scotland (S. 12. 1948 Act). Upon this depends whether the company must be registered in London (England and Wales) or Edinburgh (Scotland) and which country has jurisdiction over it. The actual address of the registered office within the country stated can be changed at will but the country cannot be changed. Determination of the *residence* of the company may depend upon the purpose for which residence falls to be determined, e.g. taxation, service of process, or attribution of enemy character in time of war. Company law places no restriction upon a registered company's main activities being carried on outside Britain.

Comparison
224 Self-evident.

CAPITAL

Dutch law
225 The Dutch Commercial Code distinguishes three forms of capital:

(i) *authorised capital,* i.e. the maximum capital which can be issued under the prevailing Articles of Association;
(ii) *issued capital,* i.e. the amount of capital which in fact has been subscribed (this amount may at no time represent less than 20% of the authorised capital);
(iii) *paid up capital,* i.e. the capital value which has been paid–in cash or otherwise–in respect of the issued capital. Unless at least 10% of the issued capital has been paid up, the directors remain jointly and severally liable for the company's obligations.

There is no absolute minimum requirement for authorised or issued capital. However, the Ministry of Justice requires that the company's issued capital should be appropriate in view of the company's object.

English law
226 In the first place a similar distinction is drawn between three forms of capital:

(i) *Nominal (also called authorised capital)* i.e. the capital with which the company is registered. This must be stated in the Memorandum of Association and is divided into shares of a fixed amount. This precludes the use of shares without a par value. (Because of the way in which the market value of shares can become greatly in excess of their par value, there have been suggestions in the past that it should be permissible for companies to issue shares of no par value. However the White Paper indicates that the Government does not regard this as necessary). The nominal capital may be increased or reduced and is really not 'capital' at all but an authority by the shareholders to the directors to create capital by the issue of shares as further explained in § 820 below.

(ii) *Issued capital* i.e. the total par value of the shares taken up by shareholders whether for consideration in cash or kind or as fully paid 'bonus' shares.

(iii) *Paid-up capital* i.e. the capital value paid up in cash or kind or by capitalisation of reserves in respect of the issued capital. Normal practice nowadays is for shares to be issued against payment in full, in which case the paid-up capital is, of course, equal to the issued capital.

227 In the case of a public company, business cannot be commenced until the Registrar of Companies has issued a 'trading certificate'. If the company has issued a prospectus, this certificate will only be granted if shares to the amount of the 'minimum subscription' have been allotted, if they are shares payable wholly in cash.

The minimum amount payable *on application* for a share (rather than later) is 5% of the nominal value (S. 47. 1948 Act). For this purpose the minimum subscription is the minimum amount as stated in the prospectus which, in *the opinion of the directors*, must be raised in order to provide for the price of any property purchased or to be purchased out of the proceeds of the issue, any preliminary expenses and underwriting commissions, repayment of monies borrowed by the company in respect of any of the foregoing and the working capital. Failure to raise the minimum subscription within 40 days of the issue of the prospectus has the consequence that all money received from applicants must be returned. The directors become personally liable to make repayment of any money not repaid by the company within a further 8 days (S. 47. 1948 Act). If a public company has not issued a prospectus there is not even this minimum subscription requirement, although in either case every director must pay to the company the amount due on all the shares taken or agreed to be taken by him, which are payable in cash. (This is not to say that every director must be a shareholder; this is not required unless the Articles of Association provide that every director must hold a minimum number of shares.) If a public company purports to enter into a contract before the trading certificate has been issued, this does not make the directors personally liable but, until the passing of the European Communities Act the contract would only become binding on the company if and when a trading certificate was granted, when it would at once become binding. However, it may be that S. 9(1) of the European Communities Act has modified this rule, and for the reasons explained in § 314 below, it is unusual to form a company as a public company.

Comparison

228 There is no requirement as to a minimum par value of shares under English law, even shares of as little as ½p being permissible, although unlikely. Dutch law lays down no maximum or minimum par value for any class of shares, but in practice shares in a BV virtually always have a par value of Dfl. 1,000. NV's usually have a Dfl. 1,000 par value as well, unless they are listed. In that case a tendency is shown in the direction of smaller par values–a par value of Dfl. 10 being the lowest known at present–in order to make dealings easier and to reach a larger investing public.

SUBSCRIPTION

Dutch law

229 In principle payment for shares is in Dutch currency. If, however, payment in kind or in a foreign currency is envisaged, this should either be provided for in the Articles of Association or any contract to that effect should be attached to the Articles of Association (Artt. 40a and 57r K).

230 If subscription in kind is envisaged upon the formation of the company, the Ministry of Justice requires to see the contract to that effect. It also requires that the value of the subscription should be defineable and that this value at least equals the par value of the issued shares. Subscription in kind after the company has been formed may only take place without the GM's approval if the Articles of Association vest the power to enter into this type of contract expressly in the directors (Artt. 40b and 57r K). Such contracts should then invariably be mentioned in the company's accounts (Artt. 40c and 57r K).

English law

231 Normally shares are dominated in sterling but there is no prohibition in Company law against their being denominated in any foreign currency. Furthermore, provided that the company receives at least the nominal amount of the shares, there does not appear to be any reason why payment for shares denominated in sterling should not be made in a foreign currency if the directors so decide.

232 Subscription for shares either at the time of formation of the company or subsequently may be made in kind or in cash. There is no procedure for official valuation of the consideration (except for the purposes of the duty on contributions to capital referred to in § 245 below). Only if this is clearly not even equal to the nominal value of the shares might the shareholder be held liable to pay for the shares in cash. A copy of the contract relating to a subscription in kind or, if there is no written contract, then specified details of the arrangements, must be filed with the Registrar of Companies (S. 52. 1948 Act).

Comparison

233 Notable weaknesses of the English system from the point of view of creditors are firstly the absence of any 'appropriate capital' or minimum subscription requirement (except in the case of public companies) and secondly the lack of official supervision of subscription in kind. Even in the case of public companies, the decision as to what should be the 'minimum subscription' is left to the directors.

PUBLIC INSPECTION

Dutch law

234 Immediately after the formation of the company the directors are obliged to register the company's business with the local Trade Register. For as long as they have not complied with this obligation, the directors remain jointly and severally liable for the company's obligations to third parties (Artt. 36g and 57c K).

Companies (NV's and BV's) must file, inter alia, the following information:

(i) the company's name, domicile (and trade name, if any);
(ii) description of the company's business;
(iii) amount of capital authorised, issued and paid up (in cash and in kind);
(iv) personal data as to managing directors and members of the board of 'Commissarissen';
(v) its Articles of Association.

All this information is open for public inspection at the Trade Register's Office free of charge. Copies of any information are available at a moderate fee.

235 Yet another legislative result of the First EEC Directive is that all companies must include in all its letters and other documents (except telegrams and publicity material) its statutory name in full and its registered office. In letters and orders the registration number at the Trade Register must also be printed (Artt. 37c and 57c K).

236 All companies pay an annual fee to the Trade Register's Office of an amount related to the company's issued capital.

English law

237 There does not exist in Britain a Trade Register, either local or national, in which a company's business must be registered in addition to filing with the Registrar of Companies, the requirements for which are given in § 209 above. However, if the company carries on business under any name other than its registered corporate name, certain particulars must be filed with the Registrar of Business Names under the Registration of Business Names Act, 1916.

Information registered either with the Registrar of Companies or the Registrar of Business Names is available for public inspection upon payment of a small search fee.

238 In compliance with the First EEC Directive, S. 9(7) of the European Communities Act requires every company to show on all business letters and order forms its place of registration, its registration number, the address of its registered office, and, in the case of a limited company exempt from the obligation to use the word 'Limited' as part of its name, the fact that it is a limited company. There is no requirement to show share capital on such documents but if any reference is made, then it must be to paid-up share capital.

239 No annual fee is payable as such by a company. However, a company is required to file an annual return giving specified information about the company and on filing this a fee of, at present, £3 is payable. In addition to this, fees are payable on the occasion of the filing of certain other required documents.

Comparison
240 Self-evident.

DURATION

Dutch law
241 If no definite period is stated in the deed of incorporation, the company is deemed to have been formed for an indeterminable period of time (Artt. 37a and 57c K).

English law
242 In the absence of any provision to the contrary in the Memorandum or Articles, the company has perpetual life. It is, however possible to provide in the Memorandum or Articles of Association that it shall be wound up after a specified period of time. This is rare except where there are different classes of shares in the capital of the company and the rights of one of the classes are such that the benefit of them can only fully be realised on a winding-up.

Comparison
243 It is refreshing to note that for once Dutch and English law already comply with Art. 4 of the draft Second EEC Directive in this respect.

COSTS OF FORMATION

Dutch law
244 When forming a company the following costs are incurred:

(i) *Notary public;* the fees of the notary are related to the size of the authorised capital;
(ii) *Trade Register;* the entry in this Register bears costs related to the amount of issued capital;

(iii) *Capital tax;* pursuant to the 1971 Taxation of Legal Deeds Act ('*Wet op Belastingen van Rechtsverkeer*') generally 2% tax is due on the par value of the issued share capital or on the real value of the issued shares–thus including the premium value and possible goodwill–whichever represents the higher figure. Under specific circumstances–which are not material for the purposes of this comparative review–the tax rate may be 1% or, even, no tax may be due at all.

The application of the 2% rate was introduced recently as a result of the EEC Directive 69/335 of the Council, which aims at harmonizing rates of indirect taxes throughout the territory of the EEC. This Directive lays down a range for this capital tax of 1% to 2%.

English law

245 The following costs are incurred in forming a company:

(i) Fee of Commissioner for Oaths with regard to the Declaration of Compliance. It should be noted that the Commissioner takes no responsibility as regards compliance with formation requirements but merely provides an official witness of the signature of the person making the Declaration.

(ii) *Registration fees;* the amount depends on the initial nominal capital, the minimum being £20 and the maximum £68.

(iii) Until 1st August 1973 there was additionally payable a stamp duty at the rate of ½% on the nominal capital.

However with effect from the date and in compliance with the EEC Directive 69/335 this stamp duty has been replaced by a duty at the rate of 1% on the value of contributions to share capital. As no share capital need be issued at the time of formation, no capital duty need now be incurred at the time of formation.

Comparison

246 In England the formation costs, assuming little capital is initially issued, are comparatively small (£68 maximum for official fees, plus professional charges and capital duty). For companies 'off-the-shelf' (see § 315 below) the current price is about £40 for a private company with £100 capital. The Dutch costs may be very large as the notarial fees are by law related to the authorised capital on a sliding scale. Furthermore the capital duty rate is twice as great in the Netherlands as in England and in England it can be postponed since no capital need initially be issued.

CONVERSION

Dutch law

247 A BV may be converted into a NV by a special resolution of the GM to that effect. The Articles of Association and the company's name will subsequently have to be changed and the conversion has to be enacted by notarial deed (Art. 36m K). Such a deed is subject to the prior approval of the Minister of Justice.

Along similar lines a NV can be converted into a BV (Art. 57f K). If, however, in this case the NV has issued share certificates, shareholders in the newly converted BV cannot exercise their rights before these certificates have been withdrawn and destroyed by the company.

No formation of a new legal entity takes place by virtue of the conversion. It is merely a matter of the existing company acting in a new form. Therefore, no adverse tax consequences are incurred through conversion.

English law

248 A private company may be converted into a public company by altering its Articles so that they no longer contain all the three restrictions required by S. 28(1) of the 1948 Act (see § 122 above). Such an alteration is carried out by Special Resolution of the GM on the passing of which the company becomes a public company and has within fourteen days either to issue a prospectus complying with the Companies Acts or to file a Statement in Lieu of Prospectus. It should be noted that so long as the three requisite restrictions remain in the Articles of Association a company is a private company even if the restrictions are not in fact observed. However, in such a case the company is treated as if the minimum number of members required is seven instead of two (S. 29. 1948 Act). A consequence of this, if the company has less than seven members, might be to make them personally liable after six months of default, as mentioned in § 212 above. No official approval is required for the conversion but as the Resolution is a Special Resolution, it has to be filed with the Registrar of Companies.

A public company can be converted into a private company by altering its Articles so as to contain the three requisite restrictions. Again this is done by Special Resolution which must be filed with the Registrar, but no official approval is necessary.

Conversion either way creates no new legal entity and does not of itself have any adverse tax consequences.

Comparison

249 There is no real difference in principle between Dutch and English law in this respect although the procedures are different, and other differences flow from such requirements as minimum membership numbers.

III. Share Capital

301 In the previous chapter brief mention has already been made of the different types of share capital and of the way in which shares are transferred. It now seems appropriate to review in some detail the various types of shares, their transferability under varying circumstances and their subscription.

TYPES OF SHARES

Dutch law
302 A NV may issue either registered shares or bearer shares, or both. Registered shares may be represented, and bearer shares must be represented, by share certificates (*'aandeelbewijzen'*). Bearer share certificates, however, may not be issued unless the full par value of the corresponding share has been paid (Art. 38c K).

BV's are only permitted to have registered shares and no certificates can be issued. The sanction is that no shareholders' rights may be exercised on the relevant shares for the period that certificates are in circulation.

Both types of company may include in their Articles of Association provisions for various types of preference shares or for so-called 'priority' shares, which entitle the holder to a certain amount of special control (Artt. 44b and 58b K).

English law
303 So far as the Companies Acts are concerned, public companies can issue either registered or bearer shares but private companies may only issue registered shares. In either case these would be issued on share certificates. However, under United Kingdom exchange control legislation it is prohibited to issue bearer certificates except with Treasury permission and existing bearer certificates have to be deposited with institutions or persons officially authorised to hold them, such as banks and solicitors. It is therefore extremely uncommon for British companies to have bearer shares outstanding.

304 Prima facie all shares rank pari passu i.e. all shareholders participate to an equal extent in the benefits of membership. It is possible and indeed quite common for a company to have two or more different classes of share capital, such as Ordinary share capital and Preference share capital. Preference shares are normally entitled to dividend at a fixed rate and to return of their par value on liquidation, both in priority to the Ordinary Shares. The dividend rights are normally 'cumulative' that is to say if there is insufficient profit in any year to pay the dividend, the amount for the following year will be the aggregate of the two years and so on. 'Participating' Preference Shares also exist and these, in addition to having a preferential dividend at a fixed rate, are also entitled to participate to some further extent in the profits. Preference Shares do not normally carry any rights to vote at GM's unless the business affects their rights or, frequently, their dividends are in arrear. It is also possible to have Ordinary Shares without voting rights, in other words they participate in the same way as normal Ordinary Shares in profits and on a return of capital on liquidation but the holders are not entitled to vote. This type of share has been used in the past in order to preserve power in the hands of a group of shareholders (obviously those holding 'normal' Ordinary Shares) but has attracted adverse publicity. There is an indication in the White Paper that the Government may legislate to restrict or prevent the use of non-voting ordinary shares.

305 Where there are different classes of shares in the capital of the company it is common to provide that their rights cannot be varied except with the approval of that class. The Articles of Association normally provide that such approval can be given by a Resolution passed at a meeting of the relevant class of shareholders and therefore it is possible for a specified majority of shareholders of that class who vote at the meeting, whether in person or by proxy, to bind the other members of that class.

Comparison

306 In NV's bearer shares are usually more important than registered shares but they are very rare in England. The reason for controlling their issue is the difficulty of controlling their transfer from resident to non-residents and vice-versa for exchange control purposes.

SHARE REGISTER

Dutch law

307 The BV's directors keep a share register in which a record is kept of all registered shareholders, payments and transfers. All notices from the company to registered shareholders are sent to the address mentioned in the register (Art. 57k K). A NV is only obliged to keep a share register of shares which are not yet fully paid up (Art. 39 K).

English law

308 As explained in § 303 above bearer shares cannot now be issued without Treasury permission. As regards registered shares, S. 110 of the 1948 Act requires a Register of Members to be kept either at the company's registered office or at some other place within the country of incorporation. Notice must be given to the Registrar of Companies of the place where the Register is kept unless this has always been at the registered office. The Register is kept up to date by the Secretary of the company on the authority of the Board of Directors (S. 110. 1948 Act).

309 The Register of Members is prima facie evidence of any matter directed or authorised by the 1948 Act to be inserted therein but is not conclusive evidence. The

Register may be inspected by members without charge and by other persons on payment of a small fee. There is also the right to require copies to be provided on payment of a fee (S. 113. 1948 Act). Notices from the company to registered shareholders are sent to the address shown in the Register.

310 Companies registered in England may not take notice of any trust affecting any shareholding (S. 117. 1948 Act) and no such notice may be entered in the Register. Articles of Association normally go further and provide that the company is only entitled to recognise the ownership of the registered holder. There are three exceptions to this rule:

(i) The Board of Trade has power to appoint an inspector to investigate and report on the membership of a company and such inspector may be given authority to require information regarding the beneficial ownership of shares (for example, where the registered member holds them on trust for another person who is the beneficial owner)–S. 172. 1948 Act, and see also § 908 below.
(ii) A company is obliged to keep a Register of Directors' Interests and this must include shares held in trust for directors (S. 27–29. 1967 Act and see § 909 below).
(iii) Companies having share capital listed on a Stock Exchange must keep a Register of substantial individual interests in which is entered information received by the company pursuant to obligations contained in the 1967 Act (S. 33–34). Such interests are notifiable to the company whether or not they are registered. See further in § 135 above.

At present an interest is substantial if it is 10% or more of the issued share capital of a class carrying rights to vote in all circumstances at GMs. The White Paper reveals that the Government proposes to reduce that figure to 5% at the most and to shorten the period for notification from the present period of fourteen days to the minimum practicable. The changes proposed by the White Paper are intended to counteract 'warehousing' which is the colloquial name for a situation in which a number of parties co-operate without disclosing that fact and each acquires an interest below the notification level in the 1967 Act, usually with the object eventually of making a take-over bid when the joint position is so strong that resistance will be difficult, if not impossible. It is also proposed that a company should have a right reasonably to demand to know who are the beneficial as opposed to the registered owners of its shares. It seems that this would not be a right automatically available, but only where the company had a good reason for needing to know, for example if it suspected a bid to be approaching or 'warehousing' to be taking place.

Comparison

311 Although an English public or private company must keep a share register under all circumstances, the Dutch NV need only do so as long as the shares are not fully paid up. The consequence of the wording of Art. 39 K is that shares may be permitted to disappear from the register once they are fully paid, unless the Articles of Association provide otherwise.

The Register of Directors' Interests has a faint echo in the Netherlands in the requirements that holders of 'incorporation shares' (issued free to incorporators but treated as fully paid up on issue) must be named in the deed of incorporation and the annual accounts (Artt. 40c and 57r K; Artt. 20d–21 WJ). It should be noted however that this type of share will have to disappear on implementation of the draft Second EEC Directive (Art. 10). There is no Dutch equivalent of the register of substantial shareholdings.

PAYMENT FOR SHARES

Dutch law

312 As mentioned above in § 225, at least 10% of each share issued must be paid up at the time of the formation of the company. As regards the remaining sum no shareholder can be released from his duty to pay in full the par value of his shares, except where in the meantime reduction of share capital has taken place (Artt. 38a and 41c; and 57h and 57r K).

As long as full payment has not taken place, the directors are under an obligation to make reference to the amount due in the share register (Art. 39 K). Usually the directors are granted the right in the Articles of Association to call upon the shareholders for the payment of (part of) the remaining sum at any time. It is thought, however, that where such a provision is omitted, the power to call for payments is exclusively vested in the GM.

Also the Receiver in bankruptcy has the right to call for and collect the outstanding amounts (Artt. 38e and 57j K). Under no circumstances may the liability to pay in full be set off against any shareholder's claim on the company (Artt. 38a and 57h K).

If the NV, contrary to the requirements of Art. 38c K, nevertheless issues certificates for partly-paid bearer shares, any subsequent purchaser who has no knowledge of the lack of payment is protected against claims for payment by the company (Art. 38d K).

English law

313 Apart from the minimum subscription requirements for public companies referred to in § 227 above, there are at present no requirements under English Company law as to minimum capital or subscription. However, one of the proposals in the White Paper (see § 126 above) is that public companies should have a minimum paid-up capital of, possibly, £10,000. The Government has not yet decided whether private companies should also be obliged to have a minimum capital.

314 Because of the minimum subscription and trading certificate requirements, the normal practice when it is eventually desired to have a public company is to form a private company and only convert it to a public company when necessary. (The simple procedure for this was explained in § 248 above). Unless a greater capital is required for trading or prestige reasons, it is usual for a company to be incorporated with a nominal capital of only £100 which can subsequently be increased in accordance with the requirements of business. Historically part of the reason for this may be found in the fact that stamp duty was payable on the nominal amount of the capital even if unissued. With the change in the system of duty referred to in § 245 above, it may now become the practice to form companies with a larger nominal capital initially, although the fact that the registration fees referred to above remain assessed by reference to nominal rather than issued capital will still constitute some discouragement to formation of companies with a larger nominal capital than is initially required for their businesses.

315 It is not necessary for any of the capital to be paid up at the time of formation of the company since as a minimum those who form the company need only *agree* to subscribe for one share each and it is permissible that they subsequently renounce their rights of subscription in favour of another person. As a result it is very common in England for company formation agents to carry on the business of forming companies in advance of known requirements and to sell them 'off-the-shelf' to persons requiring companies who are thereby saved the delay and trouble inherent in forming a company themselves. However, the White Paper indicates that this practice may possibly be counteracted in the new Companies Bill.

Shares may be issued only partly paid up and the balance may, depending upon the Articles or the terms of issue, be payable by fixed instalments or in response to calls made by the Board of Directors. The former is the normal modern practice and shares do not usually remain partly paid for any considerable length of time. The amount paid or agreed to be considered as paid on a share must be entered in the Register of Members (S. 110. 1948 Act). Reduction of capital in the meantime, which is dealt with in § 816 below, can result in the cancellation of liability to pay the outstanding amount.

Comparison

316 Both Dutch and British law will have to be altered on the implementation of the draft Second EEC Directive which in Article 7 requires that at least 25% of the par value must be paid up when the issue is for cash and the full par value when the issue is for subscription in kind. Dutch law partially meets these requirements by a 10% requirement for cash and the Ministerial Directives requiring full payment as regards subscription in kind (see § 230 above). In the case of English law, the combination of Art. 7 of the draft Second EEC Directive with Art. 6 of it (minimum issued capital) might result in the disappearance of the 'off-the-shelf' company, even if this has not already been caused by the implementation of the White Paper proposals referred to above.

TRANSFERABILITY

Dutch law

317 Together with the restriction to issuing only registered shares, another characteristic of a BV is the limitation of transferability of its shares, the reason for these requirements being to preserve the private and close nature of the company. A person who wants to have a free market in a company's shares should resort to the NV-form as the appropriate way to involve more shareholders–varying in number and background–in the financing of his undertaking.

In Art. 57l K the minimum restrictions on transfers of BV shares are set out along the lines mentioned above in § 119.

The restrictions on the transferability, however, may never be of such a strict nature that transfers are made virtually impossible or extremely difficult.

318 Registered shares are transferable by means of a deed of transfer and either serving this deed on the company or the company acknowledging the transfer (Artt. 39a and 57m K). Bearer shares are transferable by handing over the share certificate. These rules apply equally to fully paid shares and to partly-paid shares; the only difference being that after transfer of the latter the former holder remains liable for payment to the company. This liability may be partly waived by the directors and the board of 'Commissarissen'. In that case the liability only applies to calls for payment within one year after the date of transfer (Artt. 39b and 57n K).

319 By virtue of the Stock Exchange Decree ('*Beschikking Beursverkeer 1947*') a general requirement exists that all transactions involving securities (whether listed or not) must be completed through the intermediary of a Member of a Stockbrokers Association, unless the Minister of Finance has granted an exemption. In the case of transfer of securities of non-listed companies this exemption will be granted as a matter of course. If the exemption is available no share transfer tax (rate 0,12%) pursuant to the Taxation of Legal Deeds Act will be due. Issues of new shares, also those to be listed on the Stock Exchange, fall outside the scope of this Decree.

English law

320 As explained in §§ 122–123 above a private company must restrict the transfer of its shares but there is no requirement as to minimum restrictions on transfer. The White Paper contains a proposal that if directors refuse to register a transferee, they must provide him, within twenty eight days of his applying for registration, with a statement setting out the reasons why it is not in the interests of the company that he should be registered. If they fail to do so they would be required to register him. An applicant who considered the reasons given open to challenge could apply to the Court for rectification of the register. It is not entirely clear whether the Government intends that these new provisions should apply even if, as is frequently the case, the Articles of Association provide that the directors need not give any reasons when refusing registration of a transferee.

321 Registered shares, if fully paid, may be transferred by a 'stock transfer form' which need not be executed by the transferee or witnessed and may (except where the transferor is a company) be executed merely under hand as opposed to under seal (S. 1. Stock Transfer Act). This method overrides any additional requirements contained in the Articles of Assocation, although if the requirements of the Articles are followed this is also valid. The method under the Stock Transfer Act does not apply to partly-paid shares which must be transferred in accordance with the Articles of Association of the company, which may include a requirement that it be by deed (i.e. an instrument under seal) and that it be signed and sealed by a transferee.

322 After execution of the transfer it must be duly stamped (at the rate of 1 % on the value) and it is then presented to the company together with the share certificate for registration of the transfer.

Comparison
323 Self-evident.

DEPOSITARY RECEIPTS

Dutch law
324 A common phenomenon in Dutch company practice is the existence of registered or bearer Depositary Receipts for shares(' *Certificaten*'), which are usually, although not necessarily, created on the initiative of the company or with its consent.

Administration Offices ('*administratiekantoor*') hold shares and issue a receipt for each share. The Administration Office–normally in consultation with the company concerned–determines the terms of the issue and the rights of the Receipt-holder. The principal right consists of the holder's claim against the Administration Office for an amount equal to the dividend paid by the company to the Administration Office (less some administration costs).

325 The idea behind these Depositary Receipts is mainly as follows. In the first place they are thought to remedy the principal difficulties in the trade in foreign shares on the Amsterdam Stock Exchange, for example that their value is too great or that they perhaps are not bearer securities. A second motive, which is more important for Dutch practice, lies in the fact that through issue of Depositary Receipts the voting rights of the underlying shares is centralised in one place, the Administration Office, which is supposed to be well disposed towards the company. Apart from resulting in a concentration of power, it is thereby also usually intended to prevent any unwanted shareholdings or even undetected take-overs. A third effect, obviously, is that the actual investors do not have a direct say in the running of the company so that the directors and 'Commissarissen' preserve a certain independence.

326 Three types of Depositary Receipts are commonly known: convertible, partly convertible or non-convertible.

Convertible Receipts can be handed over to the Administration Office at any time in exchange for the actual underlying shares.

Partly convertible Receipts are exchangeable at the Administration Office in accordance with the Office's terms of issue, which are, sometimes, laid down pursuant to and in combination with the restrictions in shareholdings set out in the company's Articles of Association. Such a restriction may e.g. be that no shareholder other than the Administration Office can, directly or indirectly, have more than 2% of the company's issued share capital, which then in practice means that only so many Receipts are convertible into shares as represent this limit of 2%. As the Administration Office usually holds the vast majority of the shares, the result is that no individual shareholder is capable of ever exercising power of any significance in the GM. Finally, non-convertible Receipts are at no time exchangeable against their underlying shares. This last type of Receipts generally meets opposition as they undermine completely the position of the shareholder in his company.

As stated above Depositary Receipts may be registered or issued to bearer. Whereas the NV may be involved in the issue of both types of Receipts, the BV can only issue registered Receipts (Art. 57p K). The sanction for the infringement of this article is simply that so long as any bearer Receipts are outstanding, no shareholder-rights can be exercised in relation to the underlying shares.

327 Holders of Depositary Receipts may be present at GM's (Artt. 44a and 58 K) and may even have the right to speak at such meetings. However, they have no voting rights. It is, however, generally expected that the Administration Office in exercising its voting power will take into account the legitimate interests of the Receipt holders.

English law and Comparison

328 There is no provision in English Company law for the issue of depositary receipts. There is a comparable phenomenon in the case of some shares of foreign companies listed on The Stock Exchange in the United Kingdom. This arises where the market value of the shares has become so large as to hinder the flexibility of the market in them, but the company is unable by reason of its domestic legislation to sub-divide the shares into smaller units. In such a case a bank or other institution will accept deposits of the shares and against them issue receipts for a specified fraction of them. The market can then deal in these receipts which will have a practicable market value.

It is, in a way, remarkable that Dutch law virtually stands on its own as far as Depositary Receipts are concerned. The other Member States of the EEC do not recognise the concept either (with the very limited exception of France's 'Certificats Pétroliers', issuable by the Régie Nationale).

IV. Loan Capital

DEBENTURES

Dutch law

401 An important means of financing takes place through the issue by companies (both NV's and BV's) of debenture-loans (*'obligatielening'*) which are large scale loans, divided in equal parts, for each of which parts a debenture is issued to the investor. Although Dutch practice usually involves bearer debentures, registered debentures may be issued as well. After the issue of the debenture loan the company is under the obligation to file with the Trade Register yearly a statement of the number of debentures in circulation at the time (Art. 15 Hrgw.).

Debentures are normally issued under the form of a trust. In such a case the trust deed contains provisions concerning meetings of debenture-holders.

English law

402 Under English law a method of finance for a company in addition to the issue of shares is the issue of loan capital. In loan capital the basic distinction is between *secured* and *unsecured* borrowings. Secured borrowings may further be divided into those secured by a fixed charge, i.e. upon particular property, or by a floating charge, which is a type of security which exists only for borrowings by companies. The nature of a floating charge is that it 'floats' over the property which it is intended to affect until some event occurs which causes it to settle and fasten on the subject of the charge. Subject to any restrictions imposed by the terms of the borrowing, the company remains free to deal with the property over which the floating charge exists until the occurrence of the specified event which causes it to become a fixed charge (e.g. liquidation or failure to repay). Accordingly a floating charge is normally on a class of assets of a company whether present or future, the class being one which in the ordinary course of the business would change from time to time.

403 S. 455 of the 1948 Act defines 'Debenture' as 'debenture stock, Bonds and any other securities of a company whether constituting a charge on its assets or not'. However, normal usuage is 'debentures' or 'debenture stock' when the borrowing is secured, 'mortgage debenture' when there is a fixed charge and 'loan' or 'loan stock' when the borrowing is unsecured. Both private and public companies can, and do, issue loan capital but the use of trustees and a trust deed is normally confined to public companies, being required in order to protect the rights of a large number of holders. In the case of private companies, an issue of loan capital is normally to a single person or company or possibly to a small number of them. (It will be recalled that the Articles of Association of a private company will prohibit any invitation to the public to subscribe for its debentures as well as its shares; see § 122 above.)

404 Bearer debentures are subject to the same restrictions under exchange control legislation as bearer shares and are therefore uncommon in British practice.

405 If the borrowing involves the creation of a charge, whether fixed or floating, on the property of the company, it must in most cases be registered within twenty-one days of its creation with the Registrar of Companies and the registered particulars are thereafter available for public inspection (S. 95. 1948 Act). Failure to register within this time makes the charge void as against the creditors or a liquidator of the company, but it remains valid as against the company itself. A debenture which does not create a charge does not have to be registered.

The Articles of Association of a company normally provide that the directors may exercise its borrowing powers but this is frequently made subject to a specified maximum amount, often by a reference to a multiple of the issued share capital or of the issued share capital plus the reserves.

406 As mentioned above, where it is expected that there will be a large number of holders, loan capital will normally be constituted by a trust deed and this is required by the regulations of The Stock Exchange if the loan capital is to be represented by listed securities. Trust deeds are normally of considerable length and contain detailed provisions setting out the rights of the debenture holder, containing covenants by the company as to the way in which it will conduct its business, and providing for information to be given to the trustees and the holders, meetings of holders and many other matters.

If not constituted under a trust deed, the terms are normally set out either in a loan agreement, in a loan note (which may be transferable) or in what is known as a 'Deed Poll' which is a deed (i.e. a document under seal) to which the company alone is a party but which creates rights in favour of the holders for the time being.

Comparison

407 The requirement under English law to register charges, whether fixed or floating, on the property of the company with the Registrar of Companies, makes it worthwhile dealing in outline with Dutch methods to secure borrowings of a company.

The two ways of securing a borrowing which are known under Dutch statutory law are:

(i) The mortgage ('*Hypotheek*') on the company's real property. A mortgage is registered in the Mortgage-Register, in which all data relating to real property whether of companies or of individuals is found. In addition thereto the company has to disclose the mortgage in its accounts (Art. 17 WJ); and

(ii) The pledge ('*pand*') of shares. Although, in principle, pledging of shares is possible, and the company could for instance even pledge those shares which it acquired in itself, this concept hardly ever occurs. Whenever used, the pledge has to be disclosed in the company's accounts.

408 Apart from these two statutory ways of giving security, in practice another method has developed and is commonly used: 'The security-transfer of property' ('*Eigendomsoverdracht tot zekerheid*'). The 'Security-transfer' is known in various forms, inter alia, in the form of transfer of shares. In that case the transferee holds the shares and has the right to exercise all powers related to them until the company has repaid its debts. After that the shares have to be re-transferred to the company.

409 A more usual form of the 'security-transfer', however, is the transfer of all the company's current stock and debtors, whether present or future. This concept may be thought to be similar to the 'floating charge' under English law, as it is also meant to uphold the company's freedom to continue its business, using the stock and recovering the invoices, which in fact have been transferred, until some specified event results in the company having to redeem its debts to the secured creditor immediately. If it fails to do so, the creditor, having the 'security-title' to the stock and the debtors, may seek to obtain repayment of his loan by selling the stock and collecting all debts outstanding himself.

410 The basic difference from the 'floating charge' lies, however, in the question of publicity. In the case of the 'security transfer', the company has to disclose the transfer in its accounts as a 'special financial obligation' (Art. 25 WJ) but that is all there is to it. If, therefore, during the current financial year the company undertakes a 'security-transfer' for the benefit of one creditor, the remaining unsecured creditors may only come to know of their decreased chances of recovering their money, if they ask the company or learn of the transfer by chance.

Otherwise, the creditors only learn of the 'security-transfer' in the case of NV's, because these companies have to publish their accounts, and in the case of those BV's who also have to publish their accounts. BV's exempted from publication are therefore in a position to secure certain loans without the knowledge of all their creditors.

CONVERTIBLE DEBENTURES

Dutch law

411 It occasionally occurs that a company issues convertible debentures. Holders of these debentures are granted the right–under certain conditions–to exchange their debentures for shares in the company.

Any company wishing to issue such convertible debentures can only do so in compliance with the provisions concerning the issue of shares as laid down in the Articles of Association.

It goes without saying that it is essential that the number of debentures to be converted into shares can be accommodated within the margin between authorised and issued capital as from the moment of the loan.

Generally, in the case of convertible debenture loans, a trustee is appointed, whose powers are laid down in detail. The company is not free unilaterally to change the conditions of conversion, unless it has explicitly reserved the right to do so. In practice, this means that unilateral changes in favour of the debenture-holder can always be made, subject to the consent, required under the Articles of Association, of those who also have the power to decide on the issue of new shares.

Under no circumstances may the conversion of a debenture into a share take place at a price lower than the par value of the share because this practice would fall foul of Artt. 38a and 57h K, which state that no shareholder can be released from the duty to pay in full the par value of his share.

English law

412 It is quite common for listed companies to issue loan capital convertible into shares and this may be secured or unsecured. Unlisted companies may also do so, but this is not so common.

The conversion rights are set out in detail in the trust deed and normally provide for conversion at the option of the debenture holder at some time in the future. The conversion rate is initially specified but will normally be subject to adjustment in the event of certain variations in share capital. There will also be provisions protecting the rights of conversion and conversion may be permitted earlier in certain events.

The trust deed will normally also contain an obligation upon the company to keep a sufficient margin of authorised but unissued capital to cover all the conversion rights and also one to prevent shares being issued on conversion at less than their par value, which is in principle not allowed (see § 820 below).

Comparison

413 Self-evident.

TRANSFER OF DEBENTURES

Dutch law

414 Dutch Company law does not provide for any special rule as regards the transfer of debentures. Therefore, according to the general rules of passing title, bearer debentures are transferred by handing over the document. A registered debenture is transferred by deed under hand, which has to be signed by the transferor.

English law

415 Bearer loan capital is of somewhat academic importance for the reasons stated above. Registered loan capital when fully paid, can be transferred in the same way as shares under the provisions of the Stock Transfer Act (see § 321 above).

Comparison

416 Self-evident.

V. Administration and Management

Dutch law

501 The power to determine the company's course of action is divided between the Management ('*directie*'), the GM, the Board of 'Commissarissen' (if any), and the Works Council (if any). In this chapter we are basically concerned with the functioning of the Management and the Board of 'Commissarissen', whereas the GM and the Works Council will be dealt with in the following two chapters.

Management

502 The Company law provisions on management apply to both NV's and BV's. The management consists of one or more directors ('*bestuurders*'), the first of whom are appointed by the incorporators of the company upon its formation. There is no legal limitation as to the number of directors, nor any restriction as to their nationality or residence, although the Articles of Association may require certain qualifications (e.g. nationality).

503 The directors are charged with the entire day-to-day management of the company, with the administration of its assets and liabilities and with its representation in court or otherwise (Artt. 47 and 58c K).

If there is more than one director (depending on the requirements of the Articles of Association) the company is represented in its contacts with third parties by each of the directors, unless the Articles of Association state that the general powers of representation are vested in two or more directors or with a specific director (Artt. 47a and 58c K).

504 Theoretically the management's powers cannot be restricted by shareholder's directives, or otherwise. In practice, in the case of 'groups' or 'majority participations', parent or holding companies do issue instructions, which are followed by the management of subsidiaries. Instructions to the effect that the directors shall not enter into certain lines of business, or into certain contracts, without the prior approval of the GM quite often feature in Articles of Association but are not effective vis-à-vis third parties. Of course, any director acting without the required consent would be likely to get into difficulties and might find himself being dismissed for non-observance of these provisions.

Provisions in Articles of Association which provide that the company will only be bound to third parties by the signature of one specific director or by the joint signature of two or more directors, are not effective as regards these third parties, unless duly registered in the Trade Register.

Board of 'Commissarissen'

505 Again, apart from the structure provisions compulsory in 'large' companies, having a board of 'Commissarissen' is optional. Articles of Association–both of NV's and BV's–providing for such a board, usually assign to the GM the right of appointment and dismissal of board members at discretion. Here, as well, there are no restrictions as to the number or the nationality of board members.

The board, consisting of one or more members, usually functions collectively. Under certain circumstances special powers may be granted to the board's chairman or to a specifically designated member.

The board supervises the management's policy and the company's course of business. In connection therewith it advises the management (Artt. 50 and 58c K). In the exercise of their duties the 'Commissarissen' have to further the interests of the company and its business (as possibly opposed to mere shareholders' interests).

If the Articles of Association provide for a two-tier management, it is generally provided that the board of Commissarissen takes over from the GM the rights of appointing directors, as well as the right of approval of certain contracts or lines of business. As regards the latter powers, it is emphasised again that such provisions are merely of an internal nature and cannot be used as an argument against third parties in a case where the management did not seek the board's approval.

English law

506 Registered companies in England, whether private or public, only have a single governing body, normally called the Board of Directors.

The powers given to the directors are set out in the Articles of Association which normally provide that they may exercise all powers of the company which neither the Articles nor the Companies Acts require to be exercised by the GM.

In such a case the directors have full powers of management of the company. It is normal practice, at least in large companies, for the Board of Directors to appoint one of their number as a 'Managing Director'. Several persons may be appointed as 'Managing Director', capable of acting individually or jointly, depending on the terms of the appointment.

Such an appointment is frequently provided for in the Articles of Association and if so the appointment by the directors must be made in accordance with such provisions. A Managing Director is normally given power to conduct the day to day management of the company subject to the overall direction of the Board and has a duty to keep the Board informed. Furthermore, if the Articles of Association so provide, the directors may delegate their powers to a committee consisting of a limited number of themselves and such a committee will, to the extent of the powers delegated to it, act in the same way as a full Board of Directors.

Apart from the cases of a Managing Director or a Committee of Directors, the powers of the directors must be exercised collectively.

507 Where the Articles have vested the management of the company in the directors, the shareholders cannot exercise the powers given to the directors or overrule the exercise by the directors of the powers. They could, of course, by passing a Special Resolution alter the Articles so as to remove that power from the directors and as stated in § 512 below they always have the power under S. 184 of the 1948 Act to remove any director by ordinary resolution. However, if directors have been given a discretion and act bona fide, the Court will not interfere.

Comparison

508 Directors of English companies need not be nominated until after formation whereas Dutch law requires nomination by the incorporators at the time of formation (Artt. 48 and 58c K).

APPOINTMENT AND REMOVAL OF DIRECTORS

Dutch law

509 Apart from the special structure provisions applicable to 'large' companies, generally the directors are appointed and removed by the GM at its discretion. In a good many companies however, the management is well protected by so-called 'oligarchic' clauses, i.e. clauses which limit the powers of the GM in appointing and dismissing the directors (e.g. Artt. 48a and 58c K).

510 The Articles of Association must contain provisions as to what has to be done in the case of absence or incapacity of one or more directors (Artt. 48b and 58c K). In case there are any directors remaining, they will carry on with their task without there being any necessity to take further measures. If, however, no director is left or if the remaining directors cannot pursuant to the Articles of Association represent the company (see § 503 above), usually one of the company's 'Commissarissen' (if any) temporarily fills the vacancy. It is not uncommon that the Articles of Association themselves provide a procedure for temporary replacement (e.g. through appointment by the GM).

All replacements end, whenever the body of the company which has the power to do so has appointed a new director, or, whenever the absent director returns to his post.

English law

511 The first directors may be named in the Articles of Association but it is common for the Articles instead to contain a power for the incorporators of the company to appoint them. In the absence of this a majority of the incorporators may appoint them in writing. Subsequent directors are appointed in accordance with the provisions of the Articles except that in the case of a public company, as mentioned in § 124 above, not more than one director can be appointed by a single Resolution unless there has first been passed unanimously a Resolution that it can so be done. This is in order to enable shareholders to reject one director without being obliged to reject all of them

(S. 183. 1948 Act). The existing directors are frequently given power under Articles of Association to fill a vacancy caused by a premature retirement or death of a director and a person so appointed is normally subject to re-election at the next AGM. Except normally in the case of a private company the Articles of Association provide that a proportion of the directors shall retire each year but shall be entitled to offer themselves for re-election. A director may resign at any time.

512 Under S. 184 of the 1948 Act, the GM has power to remove a director before the expiry of his term of office and this power cannot be taken away by anything in the Articles of Association or any agreement between the company and the director. The Articles cannot validly require a Special Resolution for the removal of a director, although it is possible for certain shares to have greater voting rights if removal of a director is proposed. It is one of the most important powers given to shareholders under English Company law. The only exception is a director of a private company who held office for life in 1945. This is therefore not now of much significance. It should be noted however that exercise of the power of removal may constitute a breach of contract with a director giving rise to a claim for compensation. The Articles of Association may stipulate both maximum and minimum numbers of directors. The Companies Acts stipulate only minimum numbers as follows: a public company registered on or after November 1st, 1929 must have at least two directors and any other public company and any private company must have at least one director. Every company must have a Secretary who may also be director unless he is the only director (S. 176–7. 1948 Act). As to the functions of the Secretary, see further in § 515 below.

Disqualification of Directors

513 Except with the authority of the Court, an undischarged bankrupt cannot act as a director and furthermore the Court, in cases of fraud or breach of duty to the company, may disqualify a person from being a director for a period of up to five years. The Articles of Association of the company may impose an additional restriction such as the holding of a specified number of shares or as to nationality. There is a proposal in the White Paper that the Court's power to disqualify a director should be extended to cases of any offence involving fraud or dishonesty (whether or not in connection with a company) or where a director has persistently failed to comply with the Companies Acts or has acted in an improper or reckless manner (but not necessarily a fraudulent one) in relation to the affairs of the company.

514 Directors of English companies hold office for the period determined at the time of their appointment or as laid down in the Articles of Association. A common provision in the Articles is that one third of the directors shall retire each year, and those who retire shall be the ones who have held office for longest since their last appointment. Thus a director would normally hold office for three years under this system.

Comparison

515 Dutch law has no requirements as to number of directors for any type of company unlike English law. The requirement that an English company have a *Secretary* is stated above. As Dutch Company law has no equivalent requirement it may be of interest to explain his function in an English company.

The *functions of a Secretary* of a company are administrative rather than managerial, although they are not specified in the Companies Acts. No professional qualifications are required of the Secretary, although Secretaries, particularly of larger companies, frequently possess such qualifications. It is apparent from the Companies Act that the Secretary is the officer expected to ensure that the company's affairs are carried out in accordance with the law, although legally his is not the sole responsibility for this since, generally speaking, the directors are also responsible. It is possible for a company to have several Secretaries as joint Secretaries. The power of appointment and dismissal of a Secretary is normally given to the directors under the Articles of Association. Although formerly a Secretary could not by virtue of his office bind the company as regards third parties, by a recent Court decision it was recognised that in his administrative duties he does have ostensible authority to bind the company by contracts relating to administrative as opposed to managerial matters and it is, of course, always open to the Board to allow him either express or implied authority to bind the company.

516 There are no specific provisions in the Netherlands as to qualification of directors but there is of course the examination of their antecedents as related to the object of the company at the time of formation (details are to be found in the Ministerial Directives) and also the fact that foreign directors proposed for appointment on formation must be supported by a certificate of good standing. It is remarkable that these provisions have no application to any subsequent appointments.

STRUCTURE PROVISIONS

Dutch law

517 Once the company becomes of a size necessitating it to implement the structure provisions it is compulsory to have a board of 'Commissarissen', which then is vested with great powers (see § 522 below).

For these purposes the board consists of a minimum of three persons. There is no set maximum number. Pursuant to Artt. 52j and 58c K the following are not eligible to take a seat on the 'structure-board':

(i) employees of the company;
(ii) employees of subsidiaries of the company;
(iii) officials or employees of Trade Unions, which are usually involved in negotiations on employment conditions in the companies of (i) and (ii) above.

A member of this board serves for four years and can be re-elected.

Appointment

518 The way in which the members of the 'structure-board' are appointed is laid down in Artt. 52h and 58c K. 'Commissarissen' are appointed by the existing board of 'Commissarissen', unless the incorporators appointed them upon the formation of the company, or the Articles of Association did not provide for a board of 'Commissarissen' at the time that the structure-provisions became applicable to the company. In this case the first 'Commissarissen' are appointed by the GM (Artt. 52i and 58c K), whereas further appointments are then made by the board of 'Commissarissen' itself.

Both the GM and the Works Council, under these provisions, have the right to make non-binding recommendations for the appointment of new members of the board, if they so wish.

Control over appointment

519 It goes without saying that the perpetual co-option system is made subject to some form of control. In Artt. 52h and 58c K it is provided that both the GM and the Works Council have the right to object to the nomination, albeit only on the following grounds:

(i) that the candidate is not properly qualified for a position on the board, or
(ii) that if the candidate were to take his seat on the board, its composition would no longer properly reflect all interests involved. Such objections may be sustained or overruled by the SER, which hears the case on the initiative of the board of 'Commissarissen'. There is no appeal available against the SER's decision.

Dismissal

520 On demand of either the company, for these purposes represented by the board of 'Commissarissen', or a specially designated representative of the GM, or the Works Council, the Commercial Chamber of the Court of Appeal of Amsterdam may dismiss a 'Commissaris'. Grounds for such a demand are (Artt. 52k and 58c K):

(i) neglect of duty;
(ii) a radical change in circumstances so that the company cannot reasonably be required to maintain this 'Commissaris' in office; or
(iii) other important reasons.

The Commercial Chamber of the Court of Appeal of Amsterdam was specially created under the Company law reforms of 1970 and 1971 to play a role in the control and supervision of the 'public' interests of 'large' companies. Apart from its task as described in this paragraph, it is vested with the power to appoint one or more persons in order to make an inquiry into a company's state of affairs and to take appropriate measures on the basis of the outcome of such inquiry (see below in Chapter IX).

It is also the competent court in proceedings under the Annual Accounts Act, where the contents of a company's accounts may be challenged as to their compliance with the Act (see below in § 825).

Suspension

521 A 'Commissaris' may be suspended by the board of 'Commissarissen'. This suspension elapses automatically, if within one month after the board's decision to suspend, a petition for the member's dismissal has not been filed with the Commercial Chamber in accordance with the rules set out in the previous paragraph (Artt. 52k and 58c K).

Powers

522 Under the structure provisions the board of 'Commissarissen' is, to the exclusion of any other body in the company, vested with the following powers:

(i) appointment, suspension and dismissal of directors (Artt. 52l and 58c K);
(ii) adoption of the annual accounts and the accompanying explanatory note. The annual accounts will also be subject to approval by the GM, but the shareholders cannot amend the board's documents. Their only power is to approve or reject them. In the second case the board has to amend the documents in such a way that the GM gives its approval. Until such approval is obtained, no dividends may be declared (Artt. 52m and 58c K);
(iii) the board's approval is required for resolutions of the directors to (Artt. 52n and 58c K):

(a) issue, acquire, or cancel shares or debentures;
(b) co-operate in the issue of Depositary Receipts;
(c) apply for listing or de-listing of shares, debentures or Depositary Receipts;
(d) establish or terminate co-operation with another company or person;
(e) participate in other companies for a price equal to at least one fourth of the company's own issued capital and reserves;
(f) make investments of at least the amount mentioned under (e);
(g) propose any amendments to the Articles of Association;
(h) propose the company's liquidation;
(i) lay-off a considerable number of employees at once or within a relatively short period of time;
(j) change considerably the labour conditions of the company's employees.

Under the circumstances as set out in § 132 above the company may opt for the 'mitigated' structure regime, under which the powers of (i) and (ii) remain with the GM.

Government's involvement

523 It is noteworthy that Artt. 52h (12) and 58c K open up the possibility for Articles of Association to provide that one or more 'Commissarissen' are appointed by Government authorities, instead of by the board. Members of the board, however, appointed in accordance with that provision have the same powers and duties as the Members appointed otherwise. A Government 'Commissaris' is dismissed or suspended by the authority that made his appointment, notwithstanding the simultaneous application of the normal rules applicable to the other members (Artt. 52k and 58c K).

English law

524 In the White Paper, one of the issues upon which the Government is seeking views is the question of a two-tier board structure. The White Paper contains some comments upon this concept but on the whole there appears to be a preference for the continued use of non-executive directors within the existing single Board structure. By non-executive directors should be understood directors who have no executive or management position with the company but merely act as directors.

It would appear that part of the reason for preferring this to the 'continental' tendency towards two-tier boards lies in the fact that companies are financed in the United Kingdom to a much greater extent from the open market rather than by a very limited number of institutions. However the White Paper draws no definite conclusions and therefore it is as yet unknown whether a proposal will eventually be put forward for legislation on this subject.

Comparison

525 English companies, especially listed ones, frequently have one or more non-executive directors although there is no legal or Stock Exchange requirement for this. The reason is considered to be the more detached attitude and diverse experience which can thereby be applied to the company's business. This may therefore bear some similarity to the board of 'Commissarissen' under Dutch law, particularly when considered in conjunction with the normal English practice of having one or more 'Managing Directors'. Managing Directors then are responsible for the day-to-day management and the non-executive directors intervene only at the periodical Board meetings, except in cases of emergency. Major decisions, however, still have to be taken by the Board as a whole, including, of course, the non-executive directors.

526 This, also, seems the appropriate place to mention the draft Fifth EEC Directive, which deals with the structure of 'sociétés anonymes'. This draft proposes the two-tier system as an obligatory form of company management, to apply to NV's and for the time being–possibly in the same way as did the First Directive–to all English registered companies. This might only become different if and when the British Government re-defines public and private companies in such a way that the draft Directive, when adopted in the future, does not apply to all English registered companies. This would bring the English system into line with the 'continental' systems (see Art. 1 of the draft Fifth Directive) as regards the well-defined distinction between two types of company.

AGE-LIMITS

Dutch law

527 A member of the board of 'Commissarissen' retires by virtue of law not later than the day on which the AGM is held in the financial year in which he becomes 72 years. Also, nobody can be appointed 'Commissaris' at 72 years or older. This age limit may be set lower in the Articles of Association (Artt. 50b and 58c K).

There is no legal age-limit related to directors, although in practice in many Articles of Association limits are laid down (usually 65 years).

English law

528 A director must vacate office at the end of the AGM next after attaining the age of seventy and no person can be appointed a director if he has attained that age. This applies unless the Articles of Association otherwise provide or the GM appoints the director in question with knowledge of his age. It is therefore quite possible for a director to be over the age of seventy if the GM approves the appointment and these provisions do not in any event apply to private companies unless they are subsidiaries of public companies (S. 185. 1948 Act).

Comparison

529 It seems strange that, if there must be any absolute age limit, it should be applied to 'Commissarissen' rather than to directors since the former might be expected to contribute greater experience when older whereas the latter might become less able to perform detailed and full time managerial duties. The English system, under which there is no absolute bar but a requirement that the GM must re-elect the director with knowledge of his age, seems more flexible and applies whether or not a director has managerial duties.

VI. General Meeting of Shareholders

Dutch law

601 From the previous chapters it may have become clear that in a modern Dutch company–certainly in the 'large' company–the paramount role of the shareholder in determining the business of the company has been replaced by a system in which more bodies participate in the supervision, planning and determination of the company's well-being. We have already mentioned this phenomenon briefly in the first chapter, when outlining the sources of law.

The basis of this shift of power and control may be sought in changing opinions on the object and function of a company in its surrounding society. Whereas the aim in earlier years used to be the making of profits for the shareholders' benefit–since they traditionally owned the company–profit making in 1973 is not anymore the company's sole raison d'être. Factors like workers' participation, preservation of labour, protection of environment and regional policy precipitated the watering down of the GM's power–especially in the 'large' companies–in favour of power and control by those who really know what is going on (management and board of 'Commissarissen'), and together with those who, financially, usually depend on the company's continuance more than the partial investor-shareholder (i.e. the workers represented by the Works Council). As appeared from the previous chapter, the GM has a larger say in the business of a smaller company (in practice, nowadays, the BV) than in the 'large' companies, who have the obligatory implementation in their Articles of Association of the structure provisions. This chapter deals with the GM's remaining powers–varying as the case may be–and the technicalities related to them.

English law

602 Ultimately control of a company lies with the GM. In England, too, the climate of opinion seems to be moving towards the idea that a company's duties is not solely to its shareholders. For example, the White Paper stresses the duty owed to employees and to the public in general. The Government intends to publish a further consultative document later in 1973 regarding the closer involvement of employees in company affairs. For the moment, however, the power of the GM remains subject to no legal restraint nor has it to be shared with any body representing the employees.

Comparison

603 Self-evident.

POWERS

Dutch law

604 According to Artt. 43 and 58b K the GM has all powers which are not given by virtue of law or Articles of Association, to the management or to others. In this same Article we find the obligation for the management and the board of 'Commissarissen' to provide the GM with all required information unless this would be incompatible with the company's overriding interests.

Whereas in companies which do not fall under the structure provisions and which do not have a board of 'Commissarissen' the GM controls, appoints and dismisses the directors, adopts the annual accounts, decides on the disposal of profits, and, finally, takes decisions relating to changes in the Articles of Association, liquidation of the company and whatever other measures are necessary, the powers of the GM are strongly reduced under the structure regime, as will be discussed below.

605 However, even in companies (both NV's and BV's) exempted from the structure provisions, in practice, powers have partly shifted from the GM to others, mainly to the board of 'Commissarissen', if any. It is fairly common for Articles of Association to include so-called 'oligarchic' clauses, imposing restrictions on the shareholders' powers. In some cases the board of 'Commissarissen' appoint and remove the directors (Artt. 48 and 58c K). Another possibility is that the GM is only permitted to appoint directors pursuant to a binding recommendation nominating at least two persons for each vacancy (Artt. 48a and 58c K). The right to change the Articles of Association may be made subject to the approval of the holders of a special class of shares (e.g. priority shares; Artt. 45 and 58b K). Last but not least it will be recalled that by means of the creation of partly or non-convertible Depositary Receipts shareholders may even further be deprived of their natural rights.

English law

606 As under English Company law a registered company has only one Board of Directors, the GM can exercise all powers not given to the directors. However, as stated in § 506 above, the Articles of Association normally delegate to directors the exercise of all the company's powers and therefore it would be necessary for the GM to alter the Articles (requiring a Special Resolution) in order to restrict the directors' powers. As stated in § 512 above the GM has the ultimate power of being able to remove any director by Ordinary Resolution and can appoint new directors by the same method, unless the Articles of Association require a Special Resolution. There is no general obligation of English Company law for directors to provide shareholders with information beyond the specific matters required to be dealt with in the Report and Accounts (see § 826 and § 850 below). However, in the case of listed companies, The Stock Exchange imposes a higher degree of disclosure and even in the case of unlisted companies unreasonable refusal by the directors to supply information might result in a Department of Trade & Industry investigation (see § 906 below).

Comparison
607 The GM's power of removal of directors of an English company (which cannot be taken away by the Articles of Association) has no parallel in Dutch Company law since the GM only has this power over the directors if the Articles do not provide otherwise. In the absence of such a power the GM can, however, create pressure for the removal of a director by threatening removal of 'Commissarissen'. Even this 'power' has been taken away where the structure provisions apply.

STRUCTURE PROVISIONS

Dutch law
608 As discussed already in the previous chapter the GM, although not in a position to appoint members of the board of 'Commissarissen' directly, may veto any appointments on the grounds set out in § 519 above. Apart from that, Artt. 52h (4) and 58c K give the GM (as well as the Works Council and the directors) the right to make non-binding recommendations for any such appointment. It is interesting to mention that under Artt. 52h (11) and 58c K the GM may delegate the powers and duties given to it by virtue of that article and for a term determined by itself (not longer than two years) to a so-called 'Committee of Shareholders' the members of which are appointed by the GM.

The GM's powers as regards dismissal of members of the board of 'Commissarissen' are referred to in § 520 above. The GM's powers concerning the adoption of the annual accounts of 'large' companies are further discussed in the following chapter.

Under the structure provisions the GM has no formal say in the appointment of directors, which is the exclusive prerogative of the board of 'Commissarissen' (Artt. 52l and 58c K).

It will be recalled that implementation of the Artt. 52l-m K is optional in any case where the company's 'centre of gravity' is outside the Netherlands.

English law
609 No equivalent.

Comparison
610 Self-evident, and as preceding comparison.

PLACE OF MEETING

Dutch and English law
611 Shareholders' meetings of Dutch companies must be held in the Netherlands which is different from the English system, where there is no requirement under the Companies Acts that GM's be held in the country of incorporation or even in Great Britain. However, the Memorandum or Articles of Association of English companies may contain requirements in this respect.

Comparison
612 Self-evident.

AGM

Dutch law
613 At least one meeting must be held annually (*'jaarvergadering'*). The AGM has to be held within six months after termination of the company's financial year (Artt. 43a and 58b K). This term may be extended by the GM on request of the directors if special grounds justify a postponement. If no extension is granted but the requirement is nevertheless not met, directors and 'Commissarissen' are open to criminal charges and each individual shareholder will then have the right to seek authorisation from the President of the District Court to convene the AGM himself (Artt. 43e and 58b K). The AGM generally passes resolutions on the following items (depending upon the Articles of Association):

(i) appointment and removal of directors and members of the board of 'Commissarissen' (exception: 'large' companies);
(ii) adoption of annual accounts, determination of reserves and distributable profits (exception: 'large' companies);
(iii) amendment of Articles of Association (if required);
(iv) conversion and dissolution of the company (if required).

English law
614 In addition to the statutory meeting referred to in § 124 above, a registered company's first AGM must take place within eighteen months of incorporation (S. 131 (1). 1948 Act). Subsequent meetings must be held in accordance with two rules; firstly that an AGM must be held in each calender year and secondly that each AGM must be held not later than fifteen months from the date of the previous AGM. If an AGM is not held within the proper time, any shareholder may apply to the Department of Trade & Industry to call or direct the calling of the meeting. The business to be transacted at the AGM depends upon the Articles of Association and is normally declaration of dividends, consideration of the accounts and the directors' and auditors' reports, appointment of new directors and appointment and fixing of the remuneration of auditors. However, any other business can be transacted at an AGM if appropriate notice is given.

Comparison
615 There is at present under English law no equivalent of the Dutch requirement that the AGM be held within a specified period of the end of the relevant financial year. The English rules referred to above only require that AGM's are held regularly and it is indicated in the White Paper that the Government intends to create an obligation to file accounts with the Registrar of Companies within a fixed period from the end of the relevant financial year. This should help to ensure prompt holding of AGM's.

EGM

Dutch law

616 Apart from the annual meeting, an EGM may be convened at any time at the discretion of those authorised to convene a GM. All requirements as set out in § 619 and § 620 are correspondingly applicable.

Shareholders representing one tenth or more of the issued capital have the statutory right to invite the management and the board of 'Commissarissen' to convene an EGM. The shareholders have, in that case, to submit full particulars of the matters to be dealt with.

If these two bodies fail to convene a meeting to be held within six weeks after the invitation, the shareholders may seek permission from the President of the competent District Court to convene the EGM themselves on terms and conditions as laid down by the President (Artt. 43c and d; and 58b K).

English law

617 An EGM can be convened by the directors at any time. Members holding between them not less than one tenth of the paid-up capital of the company carrying voting rights may require the directors to call an EGM and if the directors fail to do so within twenty-one days the requisitionists or those holding onehalf of their voting rights may do so within three months from the expiration of the twenty-one days and may recover from the company their reasonable expenses incurred in doing so. The company, in turn, may retain the amount of the expenses out of directors' fees or remuneration which become due to those in default (S. 132. 1948 Act). In the case of urgency, a Court order may be granted to compel the directors to call a meeting immediately.

Comparison

618 If the directors fail to convene an EGM when requested by the shareholders to do so, it is necessary in the Netherlands to apply to the Court for approval (in accordance with Artt. 43c–d and 58b K), which excludes abuse by shareholders of this right, whereas in England application to Court is unnecessary and if shareholders abused their rights, the directors would probably have to apply to the Court to prevent the abuse.

CONVOCATION AND VOTING

Dutch law

619 The management and the board of 'Commissarissen' are equally authorised to convene a GM (Artt. 43b and 58b K). They must give a minimum of fifteen days notice to all shareholders, and to holders of Depositary Receipts issued with the company's co-operation, by means of an announcement in a newspaper (Artt. 43f and 58b K) or, if an NV only has registered shares and/or registered Depositary Receipts; in accordance with such method as the Articles of Association prescribe (usually through letters to the addresses appearing in the share register). Convocation letters have to be sent to shareholders in a BV (Art. 58 K). In this notice the meeting's agenda is set out. The GM can only take decisions related to items other than those featuring on this agenda if the entire issued capital is represented.

Under Artt. 43h and 58b K non-observance of the 15-days period or failure to give any notice at all, results in the invalidation of the GM's resolutions unless, again, the entire issued capital is represented. It is thought that these provisions also apply in cases where notice is not given by accident.

620 Minutes are kept of each GM. Only shareholders may cast votes. Each shareholder has at least one vote, and in general the 'one share/one vote' system is followed. All decisions are taken by absolute majority, unless the Articles of Association require otherwise. Holders of Depositary Receipts have the right to attend and speak at the GM, but they cannot vote. The Articles of Association may provide that, where no bearer shares or Depositary Receipts are issued, all shareholders, concurring in writing may pass resolutions without a meeting being held (Artt. 46b and 58b K).

English law

621 The GM's are convened on the authority of the Board of Directors. In the case of an AGM not less than twenty-one days notice must be given to all persons who, under the Articles of Association, are entitled to receive notice and also to the auditors. There is normally a provision in the Articles to the effect that accidental omission to give notice to any person does not invalidate the meeting and also that notice need not be given to members who are abroad. Resolutions can only be passed at the GM if proper notice has been given of them.

622 The normal business of an AGM is dealt with by Ordinary Resolutions which require only a bare majority of those attending and voting. Only fourteen days notice need be given of an Ordinary Resolution if it is to be proposed at an Extraordinary General Meeting. However, as mentioned above, if proposed at the AGM twenty-one days notice will have to be given. Certain matters require the passing of a Special Resolution for which the period of notice is twenty-one days and the necessary majority is three-quarters of the votes cast at the meeting. Some of the things a company can only do by Special Resolution are as follows:

(i) alteration of the objects clause in the Memorandum of Association;
(ii) alteration of the Articles of Association;
(iii) change of name;
(iv) reduction of capital.

A third type of Resolution is the Extraordinary Resolution, which must be passed by the same majority as required for a Special Resolution. The period of notice required depends upon the meeting, i.e. twenty-one days if at the AGM or fourteen days if at an EGM. Its most common use is for putting a company into liquidation but the Articles of Association may also require it for other purposes.

623 Minutes must be kept of all GM's (and of meetings of the directors)–S. 145. 1948 Act. Voting rights of GM's are in accordance with the Articles of Association (see also § 304 above).

Comparison
624 Self-evident.

QUORUM

Dutch law
625 There is no legal quorum requirement in order to hold a GM, nor, in general, does the validity of resolutions passed in such a GM depend on any quorum (Artt. 44d and 58b K). However, the Articles of Association may provide for a quorum in order to pass certain important resolutions (e.g. amending the Articles of Association, conversion, dissolution). Company law itself also requires a certain quorum for specific resolutions, inter alia resolutions overriding 'oligarchic' clauses (e.g. Artt. 43g, 43h, 44, 45 and 48a K).

English law
626 In the absence of any provision as to quorum in the Articles of Association, the minimum quorum under the 1948 Act is two in the case of a private company and three in the case of a public company, who must be personally present (S. 134). The Articles may require a higher or lower number and may permit members present by proxy to be counted for the purpose of ascertaining the quorum. In the absence of a quorum there can be no meeting and no Resolutions can validly be passed.

Comparison
627 Self-evident.

MAJORITY POWER AND MINORITY PROTECTION

Dutch law
628 In principle, shareholders may by a so-called 'voting-agreement' ('*stemovereenkomst*') undertake to use their powers in one way or other. However, such an agreement will not in some circumstances preclude them from casting their vote differently. The leading criterion for the departure from such undertaking lies in the principle that each shareholder, after his right to safeguard his personal interests, has an obligation to exercise his voting rights–and thus his powers–'in good faith' vis-à-vis his fellow-shareholders and the company.

This criterion may lead to majority-resolutions, which can be–and in fact, regularly, are–attacked in court by the minority on the grounds of 'abuse of majority-power' ('*misbruik van meerderheidsmacht*') this being contrary to the principles of good faith. If such a claim is successful the Court declares the resolution null and void.

A sensible time limit is set to the initiation of such a procedure. Nullity based on the fact that either the resolution has not been passed in a regular way, or without observing all formal requirements, except in cases of fraud, must be invoked within six months after the date of the resolution (Artt. 46a and 58b K).

This action for nullity can be started by a shareholder or by any interested third party.

English law

629 Shareholders may agree between themselves to exercise their voting rights in a particular way and this cannot be upset even if as a result the exercise of a shareholders' voting power is not in the best interests of the company. The company must recognise the vote of the registered shareholder and if he votes contrary to his contractual arrangement with another shareholder or a third person the person aggrieved has no rights against the company but only against the shareholder who was broken his contract. However this freedom will be restricted by the Courts where a majority of members are attempting to commit a fraud on the minority. No particular time limit is laid down within which an action based upon fraud on the minority must be brought as this is not a matter dealt with at all in the Companies Acts. However a Court would not tolerate an unreasonable delay in taking action.

630 Although in judgements of the English Courts it has frequently been said that shareholders must exercise their votes bona fide for the benefit of the company as a whole, in principle the shareholder of an English company may exercise his rights selfishly if he so wishes and agreements entered into by him to use his rights, including his votes, in a specified way can be enforced by Court process against him. Only if the conduct of the shareholder(s) amounts to what is called 'fraud on the minority' will the Courts interfere. This does not mean that there must be 'fraud' in its usual legal sense but rather the abuse of a fiduciary position and the sufferer need not be literally a minority of shareholders but, for example, could be the company itself. The most common examples of conduct held by the Courts to amount to 'fraud on the minority' have been wrongful expropriation by some shareholders of the company's property, improper release of directors from liability for breach of their duties to the company, and expropriation of the shares of some members of the company without adequate compensation.

631 A further aspect of minority protection in English law is that under S. 210 of the 1948 Act any member of a company who complains that the affairs of the company are being conducted in a manner oppressive to some part of the members may apply to the Court and, if the Court is of the opinion that the facts are as above and that to wind up the company would unfairly prejudice that part of the members but otherwise it would have been just and equitable to wind the company up, the Court has power to make such order as it thinks fit whether for regulating the conduct of the company's affairs in future, for the purchase of the shares of any members by other members or by the company (and in that case also for the necessary reduction of capital) or otherwise. As stated in § 907 below the Department of Trade & Industry also has power to apply to the Court in such circumstances following an investigation (S. 35. 1967 Act).

If the requirements of the Section are met the Court therefore has extremely wide powers but in exercising its discretion appears to take a somewhat cautious attitude. As a result the White Paper contains proposals to strengthen the protection given by these provisions and to enable the Court to intervene if it is shown that the affairs of the company are being conducted in a manner unfairly prejudicial, but not necessarily oppressive, to the minority and that even isolated acts failing short of *a course of conduct* should suffice.

Comparison

632 In both Dutch and English law the concepts of 'abuse of majority-power' and 'fraud on a minority' are the creation of case law. As the English system is based on the breach of a relationship of 'trust' this is thought to be rather similar to the 'good faith' principle which governs the Dutch application of the concept.

However, the practical application of the principles in either country cannot be certain as they depend on the Court's individual appreciation of commercial morality. It is also a floating concept because of the steady development in company 'philosophy'.

VII. Workers Participation

Dutch law

701 It will be recalled that in the introduction to Chapter V the Works Council was mentioned as one of the bodies of the Dutch company. From the following outline of the *Works Council Act* it will become clear that a Works Council's influence on the day-to-day management of a company which is large enough to be required to have a Works Council, is substantial.

702 It is of interest that the Act in principle applies to all undertakings (NV's, BV's and non-corporate bodies), where as a rule 100 or more are employed. Such undertakings have to establish a Works Council elected *from* those who have been employed by the company for more than three years and elected *by* those employed for at least one year. The number of members of the Works Council depends on the total number of employees (Artt. 2 and 6). The SER may exempt companies from establishing a Works Council or may require companies with 25 or more employed to have one, if it is of the opinion that this is appropriate (Artt. 3 and 4).

703 A NV or BV is required to hold at least six Works Council meetings per year under the presidency of one of the directors. At these meetings all aspects of the company's business are open to discussion and the Works Council may express its wishes and objections and proposals can be made (Art. 23). At at least one of the meetings the accounts of the company must be discussed, if the company is obliged to publish its accounts (see below §§ 830–832) or, if no such obligation exists, accounts must be submitted to a meeting in a specified minimum form (Art. 24).

704 It should be observed that, as the Act gives the Works Council the right to lay down its own procedural rules, the frequency of meetings is in fact entirely in the hands of the Works Council itself. It can therefore convene meetings as often as necessary, whereas the company only has to make sure that the minimum number of meetings is held.

705 It is of particular interest that the directors *have to* seek the Works Council's advice on a wide range of subjects, mentioned in the Artt. 25–31 of the Act. These relate to (inter alia):

- mergers and take-overs;
- lay-offs;
- changes in the company's organisation, structure, business or centre of activity;
- joint ventures;
- the company's social policy;
- pension schemes, labour hours, holidays, safety and hygiene provisions at the company's premises.

The Works Council has to be kept informed of all proposed appointments or removals of any of the company's officers, as well as of all other matters which may be of interest to it or which may improve its functioning.

706 In this respect it will be recalled that the Works Council's strongest powers lie in the rights to object to the appointment of a 'Commissaris' of a company which has implemented the structure provisions (Artt. 52h and i K) and to demand the removal of any 'Commissaris' in such a company through initiating a procedure to that end before the Commercial Chamber of the Amsterdam Court of Appeal (Art. 52k K).

707 Finally it should be observed that the Act also gave a legal basis to what had already been developed in practice for a good many years, i.e. the Central Works Council.

Groups of companies may install a Central Works Council (Art. 33) in those cases where the requirement to have Works Councils is already applicable to two or more companies in the group.

The members of the Central Works Council are recruited from the individual Works Councils of the respective companies. The Central Works Council, which lays down its own procedural rules, occupies itself with all problems related to the group of companies as a whole, and has for this purpose the same powers as the individual Works Councils have in their respective companies.

English law and Comparison

708 There is no present equivalent in English law of the Works Council requirements of Dutch law. However, under the Industrial Relations Act, 1971, S. 57, any business (not only companies) employing more than 350 persons (excluding part-time and new employees and those who ordinarily work outside Great Britain) can be obliged to give to their employees annual written statements containing specified information relating to the business. In the case of companies, this may extend to associate or subsidiary companies.

Furthermore, the White Paper states that it is in the interest of all concerned, including those who provide the capital, that the employees should have an appropriate opportunity of influencing decisions which can closely affect their own interest. It remains to be seen in what way this sentiment will be given legal effect.

VIII. Assets

Dutch law

801 This chapter aims at dealing with the maintenance of the company's capital, its increase and its reduction, the latter two items being of particular importance for the purpose of ensuring adequate protection for shareholders and for the company's creditors.

Dutch Company law does not occupy itself with the way in which the company's assets should be managed commercially. The law, however, lays down rules to preserve the capital in order to protect creditors, the capital being their only security. The shareholders' subscription should be related to the amount of capital issued and the extent of it and of any subscription in kind should be made known to outsiders. There is a prohibition against encroachment upon the capital by making undue distributions to the shareholders and, finally, rules are laid down for periodical reporting on the company's state of affairs. Below will be highlighted various aspects which may be of particular interest for the purposes of this review. Unless stated otherwise, all these rules apply equally to NV's and BV's.

English law

802 Apart, possibly, from restraining purchase of assets at an excessive value or the disposal of them at an under-value where this would constitute a fraud upon minority shareholders, English Company law does not restrict the way in which the company's assets are dealt with. It does, however, lay down requirements for the maintenance of the capital of the company by restricting the amount which may be distributed to shareholders, requiring Court approval for reduction of capital, and the regular production of directors' and auditors' reports and accounts which are filed with the Registrar of Companies and therefore available for public inspection.

Comparison

803 Self-evident.

SUBSCRIPTION

Dutch law

804 It will be recalled that subscription of capital was already briefly discussed above in § 312, where it was stated that the principle is laid down in Artt. 38a and 57h K: Under no circumstances may a shareholder be released from his liability to pay in full for the shares he has taken, unless in the meantime reduction of share capital takes place (Artt. 41c and 57r K).

English law

805 Requirements as to payment of shares are dealt with in § 313 above, there being in general no requirements under British Company law as to minimum capital or subscription.

Comparison

806 See comparison in § 316 above.

PRESERVATION OF CAPITAL

A. Dividends out of capital

Dutch law

807 The basic principle is that no distributions may be made to shareholders in such a way that the value of the company's assets sinks below the par value of the issued capital. Although in general it is not prohibited to distribute dividends out of the company's capital reserve, it is prohibited to distribute profits to shareholders at the end of any financial year if it appears, from the adopted profit and loss account for that year, that a loss has been made in previous year(s) which cannot be covered by the company's reserves nor redeemed in any other way (Art. 42e K).

For the same reason of preservation of capital it is, in general, not permitted for the Articles of Association to provide that interest will be payable to shareholders in respect of the amount of their obligatory payment for shares unless the interest is paid in the form of a dividend and therefore, subject to the principles stated in this paragraph (Art. 41 K).

Nevertheless such interest may be paid for the period that the company has not yet fully commenced trading. The rate of interest and the number of years during which the interest will be paid, has to be laid down in the Articles of Association, with a maximum of 5% and four years. This provision allows the NV to build its factory or other plants without the shareholders making an initial loss in interest on their investment.

English law

808 The Companies Acts themselves do not contain any requirement that dividends should not be paid out of capital. However, the question has been extensively considered by the Courts and as a result of judicial decisions the law, although in some respects still uncertain, appears to be that as a general principle dividends must only be paid out of profits and not out of capital or capital reserves.

There are several rules which follow from the above principle, particularly in order to determine what constitutes 'profit'. Consideration of these is outside the scope of this Review but it may briefly be noted, inter alia, that a company must not pay dividends if as a result it would not be able to pay its debts as they fall due, losses of fixed assets need not be made good before a revenue profit can be available for dividend, provision need not be made for depreciation, a realised profit on a sale of fixed assets may be used for dividend provided fixed and circulating assets exceed liabilities; and losses of previous accounting periods need not be made good before a dividend can be paid out of profits of a current year's trading.

809 The whole of the foregoing is subject (a) in law to the requirements of S. 149 of the 1948 Act that the balance sheet and profit and loss account must give a true and fair view of, respectively, the state of affairs of the company at the end of its financial year and the profit and loss for a financial year and (b) in practice to the requirements of the accountancy bodies whose members carry out the audit of public companies and many private companies.

Subject to the consent of the Department of Trade & Industry and if authorised either in the Articles of Association or by Special Resolution of the GM, a company may pay interest on paid up shares which were issued for the purpose of raising money for the construction of works, buildings, or plant which cannot be made profitable for a lengthened period (S. 65. 1948 Act). This is not dependent upon there being any profits and is therefore a statutory exception to the general principle explained above.

Comparison

810 It is interesting to note (i) that either type of Dutch company may pay dividends out of capital reserves, (ii) that the rules of Art. 41 K as to interest are not applicable to BV's and (iii) that the payment of interest on shares is expressly limited to those issued for the purposes specified in S. 65 of the 1948 Act, whereas the equivalent provision in Art. 41 K is not so limited, although Dutch practice is invariably restricted to the purposes described above in the rare cases when the provision is used at all (*'bouwrenten'*).

B. A company acquiring its own shares

Dutch law

811 Paid-up shares may be acquired for consideration by the company, but only up to the amount mentioned in its Articles of Association.

There is no legal maximum set to this amount, but in the Directives of the Ministry of Justice presently in force, the maximum is 50% of the capital issued. It goes without saying that the law prohibits the company acquiring shares which have not yet been fully paid up, since the result thereof would under Artt. 38a and 57h K be that the company would have to pay up these shares itself (Artt. 41a and 57r K). It is thought that the company might acquire fully paid shares for no consideration up to any amount as the Ministerial Directives do not contain any restriction in this respect.

812 Once the company has acquired some of its shares, it may sell them again. The advantage of this may be that the formal requirements for the issue of new shares will not have to be observed, unless the Articles of Association so require. In the meantime however, the real value of these shares should appear on the balance sheet.

Another possibility is that the company may withdraw these shares. Unless otherwise stated in the Articles of Association this would require the approval of the GM. As long as the issued capital, as stated in the Articles of Association is still present after the withdrawal no amendment of the Articles of Association will be required. It should be noted that the normal requirements for the reduction of capital (see § 815 below) do not have to be observed. Both the law and the Ministerial Directives are silent in this respect.

Yet another aspect of such acquisition concerns the rights which may be exercised on these shares. Whereas the law does not provide any rule, the Ministerial Directives require that the company cannot exercise any voting rights in respect of shares in itself acquired by it nor may these shares be taken into account in establishing any quorum required by the Articles of Association. In general, no dividend will be payable on such shares either. It is felt that these restrictions may also apply to shares acquired for no consideration (see e.g. Art. 20 of the draft Second EEC Directive).

English law

813 It has been established by case law that a company cannot acquire its own shares. Nor, except in two cases, can it redeem issued share capital. The first exception is if shares are expressly issued as redeemable. These can only be Preference Shares and can only be redeemed out of either profits or a fresh issue of shares made for the purpose of the redemption, in addition to other requirements. The second exception is in the case of a reduction of capital and this topic is dealt with in § 816 below.

Furthermore, subject to very limited exceptions, no company can be a shareholder in its holding company and any allotment or transfer of shares in a company to its subsidiary is void (S. 27. 1948 Act).

An additional restriction is that a company may not, whether directly or indirectly, give any financial assistance for the purpose of or in connection with the purchase or subscription of shares in itself or in its holding company. There are exceptions for lending in the ordinary course of business and purchase or subscription by, or by trustees for, employees (S. 54. 1948 Act).

This Section has caused considerable problems in practice, by catching innocent transactions and failing to prevent some undesirable transactions. The Jenkins report suggested that it should be modified and the White Paper indicates that some amendments may be made to it but does not particularise them.

Comparison

814 As Dutch law contains no provision forbidding or regulating mutual shareholdings, even if one of the companies involved is in control of the other, the position of minority shareholders and of creditors could be prejudiced to a large extent.

Dutch law may have to be amended in the future at least as far as subsidiaries are concerned once the EEC harmonization develops further in that respect. It is also noteworthy that Art. 47 of the Statute for the 'European Company' limits the subsidiary holding shares in its parent company to 10%.

Under Dutch law there is also no general provision restricting a company giving any financial assistance for the purpose of subscription of shares in itself or in its holding company.

C. Reduction of capital

Dutch law

815 Artt. 41c–g and 57r K provide for the rules to be observed in case of capital reduction. Reduction of capital may be achieved by releasing the shareholders from their liability to pay up shares taken by them, or through repayment upon shares, or, as is already discussed above, through withdrawal of shares acquired by the company itself (Artt. 41c and 57r K). Control of the first two ways of capital reduction is guaranteed through the requirement that for reduction purposes the authorised (but not the issued) capital stated in the Articles of Association should be amended. As will be discussed below, any change in the Articles of Association requires a declaration of non-objection by the Ministry of Justice, so that the Ministry in this case is able to check whether all formal requirements have been met. The directors of the company are under an obligation to announce the proposed reduction in both the Official Gazette ('*Nederlandse Staatscourant*') and in a local newspaper. The resolution to reduce the capital and to amend the Articles of Association has to be filed with the Trade Register as well. Within two months from the day the announcement was published, each creditor may oppose the proposed reduction (Artt. 41d and 57r K). This opposition is made by filing a reasoned petition to nullify the GM's resolution with the District Court of the place of the company's registered office. This Court then decides only after having heard all parties and such other creditors as it deems necessary. It may also hear witnesses and experts, even upon its own initiative (Art. 41e and 57r K). Appeal may be made against the District Court's decision (Artt. 41g and 57r K).

English law

816 The capital cannot be reduced unless the Articles of Association contain power to do so, which is normally the case (e.g. Regulation 46, Table A, 1948 Act). If there is no such power, it must first be obtained by amending the Articles (by Special Resolution of the GM). S. 66 of the 1948 Act then permits a company to reduce its share capital by Special Resolution in any of the following ways:

(a) Extinguishing or reducing unpaid liability on shares not fully paid-up.
(b) Cancelling paid-up share capital which is lost or unrepresented by available assets, or
(c) Paying off any paid-up share capital which is in excess of the wants of the company.

Any such Resolution is subject to confirmation by the Court. Where at the proposed reduction involves either diminution of liability in respect of unpaid share capital or payment to any shareholder of any paid-up share capital, and in any other case where the Court so directs, the following provisions will apply unless the Court thinks it proper that they should not do so (S. 67. 1948 Act):

(i) Creditors who at the date fixed by the Court are entitled to any debt or claim which, if the date were the commencement of the winding-up of the company, would be admissible in proof for the purposes of the winding-up, are entitled to object to the reduction.
(ii) The Court settles a list of creditors so entitled to object.
(iii) If a creditor entitled to object does not consent to the reduction, his consent may be dispensed with upon the company securing payment of his debt or claim.
(iv) The Court may require advertisement of the reduction and that the words 'and reduced' be added at the end of the company's name for a specified period. (S. 68. 1948 Act).

If the reduction does not involve diminution of liability or payment off of paid-up capital, the reduction is merely advertised and then heard by the Court. An Order is normally made at once since creditors have no right to object except in very special circumstances.

In any event there must be registered with the Registrar of Companies a Court Order confirming the reduction. The Registrar issues a Certificate of the reduction which is conclusive evidence of it. The reduction only takes effect from the grant of the Certificate.

It will be appreciated that, although amendment of the Articles of Association does not require any official approval and may even be unnecessary, the fact that the Registrar requires the Court confirmation before issuing his certificate ensures that the procedure laid down by the Act must be followed.

Comparison

817 In the Netherlands, despite the Ministerial control applicable to the necessary changing of the Articles, there is no effective method of ensuring that the reduction of capital will not prejudice creditors. A creditor who does not see or hear of the announcement of the reduction will not in practice be able to object since this must be done within 2 months of the announcement. The protection of creditors is better ensured under English law which in this respect meets the requirements of Artt. 29–30 of the Draft Second EEC Directive.

D. Increase of capital

Dutch law

818 Although creditors generally will not be harmed by an increase of the company's issued capital, an issue otherwise than to existing shareholders (e.g. stock-dividend) may create totally different relationships between the shareholders since original shareholders will see their voting power watered down. Probably, therefore, the power to decide upon an increase of the issued capital lies with the GM unless, by means of a provision in the Articles of Association, this power has been taken away from it (Artt. 43 and 58b K). If this is done this power is usually given to the directors. It is also contended that the directors by virtue of their general powers of management

(Artt. 47a and 58c K) have the power to decide upon an issue. It should be noted, that as far as companies which have to implement the structure provisions are concerned, the consent of the board of 'Commissarissen' is required if the directors decide to issue new shares (Artt. 57h and 58c K). It is thus suggested that for these companies such an 'oligarchic' provision in favour of the directors will be the rule rather than the exception, or, even, that in those companies the power rests with the directors.

819 An issue of new shares requires no change in the Articles of Association if the balance of the authorised capital after deduction of the number of shares already issued allows for the new issue. If not, the authorised capital will have to be increased by resolution of the GM. This constitutes an amendment of the Articles of Association, requiring the Ministerial declaration of non-objection.

New shares cannot be issued at below their par value (Artt. 38a and 57h K). Issues at above par are allowed, and, in practice, fairly common. The then existing premium value of the share ('*agio*') may be set off against a shareholder's claim on the company. The premium may also be paid back to shareholders through an issue of so-called '*bonus*'-shares or '*stock-dividend*' or even in cash if the company does not require the premium amount for the future conduct of its business. The premium on shares has to be shown as the '*agio-reserve*' on the company's balance sheet.

It should be mentioned as well that pursuant to Art. 38a (2) K a NV may issue shares at a discount of a maximum of 6% if the issue takes place through the intermediary of those who professionally undertake to procure the issue for their own account (e.g. Banks, Stockbrokers).

English law

820 Under English law the authorised capital can only be increased by the GM. However Articles of Association commonly give the directors power to issue any authorised but unissued share capital as they think fit and the directors therefore do not need approval of the GM unless there is insufficient authorised capital for the issue which they propose.

If the Articles of Association so provide, the authorised capital can be increased merely by an Ordinary Resolution. Otherwise a Special Resolution will be necessary.

In principle shares cannot be issued at a discount (i.e. below their par value). However there is one exception to this, under S. 53 of the 1948 Act, where the person to whom the shares are issued may be entitled to deduct or be paid underwriting commission (at a maximum rate of 10%) and another exception under S. 57 of that Act in order to avoid a company whose shares are quoted at below par from being unable to raise fresh capital. The procedure under S. 57 requires approval both by GM and by the Court and is rarely used.

Shares are frequently issued at above their par value and if this is done the excess must be credited in the company's accounts to a special account called 'the Share Premium Account' which cannot be distributed by way of dividend except in compliance with the provisions relating to reduction of capital dealt with in § 816 above.

Comparison

821 Both systems require share premiums to be credited to a special account but Dutch law permits what is prohibited by English law, namely distribution in cash as 'dividend' of the amount standing to the credit of that account, whether or not there are enough profits to cover the desired rate of dividend.

Apart from the different maximum rates of discount allowed on issue, under Dutch law this is only allowed to those who professionally undertake to procure issues. There is no such restriction in English law.

ACCOUNTS

Dutch law

822 There is a general book-keeping requirement for all undertakings, and also for non-corporate bodies (Art. 6 K). All books and other records have to be retained for at least ten years. Special requirements, however, are laid down in the provisions of the Commercial Code for the book-keeping of companies. Annually, within five months after expiration of the company's financial year, the directors of all NV's and BV's have to draw up a balance sheet and a profit and loss account, together with an explanatory note. All these documents have to be signed by the directors and by the members of the board of 'Commissarissen' (if any). The accounts will be adopted by the GM unless the power to do so is given to the board of 'Commissarissen', either by virtue of law or of a provision in the Articles of Association (Artt. 42 and 57r K).

English law

823 A company must keep proper books of account with respect to (S. 147. 1948 Act):

(a) All sums of money received and expended by the company including the matters in respect of which the receipt and expenditure took place.
(b) All sales and purchases of goods by the company.
(c) The assets and liabilities of the company.

The directors are obliged to lay before the company at least once in every calendar year a profit and loss account and a balance sheet. The first accounts must be laid before the GM not later than eighteen months after incorporation. The accounts must be made up to a date not earlier than nine months before the date of the meeting (twelve months in the case of a company carrying on business or having interests abroad). A director's report is required to be attached to every balance sheet laid before the GM (S. 157. 1948 Act). This is a document of considerable importance since the 1967 Act enlarged the information required to be included in it. The report of the Auditors must also be annexed to the balance sheet. As to these two reports, see further in §§ 844, 847 and 850 below.

The balance sheet and the profit and loss account must be signed on behalf of the Board by two of the directors (three in the case of a banking company, in which case the balance sheet must also be signed by the Secretary or Manager, if any)–Sections 155–6. 1948 Act. The balance sheet and the accompanying documents must, at least twenty-one days before the date of the meeting, be sent to every member of the company, every holder of debentures of the company and any other person entitled to them.

There is no legal obligation that the GM adopt or approve the accounts. The Articles of Association commonly require that they be considered however (e.g. Regulation 52 of Table A Part I).

Comparison

824 It may be considered remarkable that in English Company law there is no requirement that a company's annual accounts be adopted or approved by the GM. The 1948 Act merely requires them to be 'laid before' the GM, and Articles of Association often provide only that they should be 'considered'. This contrasts strongly with the Dutch requirement of adoption by the GM. It is theoretically possible for an English company's accounts to be filed with the Registrar of Companies without having been approved by the GM.

It should be noted that the draft Fifth EEC Directive when dealing with the powers of the GM, also speaks of adoption of the annual accounts (Art. 48). The annual accounts within the meaning of Article 2 of the draft Fourth EEC Directive (see § 828 below) must be adopted by the GM. The laws of the Member States may, however, provide that they shall be adopted by the management and the supervisory body of the company, unless those two bodies decide otherwise or fail to agree. In this way the Member States have the choice of implementing either an exclusive or an alternative competence of the GM.

CONTENTS OF ACCOUNTS

Dutch law

825 The '*Wet op de Jaarrekening van Ondernemingen*' (WJ) provides in some detail the requirements and standards which have to be observed when drawing up the accounts. The Act also lays down provisions for a procedure before the Commercial Chamber of the Amsterdam Court of Appeal in the case of any interested person being of the opinion that the company's accounts do not meet the stringent requirements set out in the Act (see Artt. 31–35 WJ).

The WJ introduced in its Artt. 13–14 a system of compulsory 'Group' accounting in that a company which holds more than 50% of the shares in another company, has to disclose in accordance with the requirements of the WJ all information related to the subsidiary. This should be done through the inclusion in the explanatory note of either consolidated accounts, separate accounts, or combined accounts of all companies concerned. Furthermore, the names and registered offices of these subsidiaries have to be stated in the accounts.

English law

826 The balance sheet must give a true and fair view of the state of affairs of the company at the end of its financial year and the profit and loss account must give a true and fair view of the profit or loss of the company for the financial year. This requirement of a 'true and fair view' is an overriding one.

Subject to this the main requirements for the balance sheet and profit and loss account are contained in the Eight Schedule to the 1948 Act which was amended by 1967 Act. The amended Schedule is set out in Schedule 2 to the 1967 Act.

Group Accounts

827 A holding company as defined below must present to its members, with its own annual accounts, group accounts relating to the state of affairs and profit and loss of itself and its subsidiaries unless it is itself a wholly-owned subsidiary.

In principle these accounts must deal with all subsidiaries unless the holding company's directors consider it would be impracticable or of no real value or would involve expense or delay out of proportion to the value to the members of the holding company.

A further exemption is possible with the approval of the Department of Trade & Industry if inclusion in the group accounts would be misleading or harmful to the business of any of the group companies or treatment as a single undertaking would not be reasonable because of differences in the nature of the business (S. 150. 1948 Act).

A holding company is one of which another company is a subsidiary whether because (S. 154. 1948 Act):

(a) The holding company is a member of it and controls the composition of its Board of Directors, or
(b) the holding company holds more than half in nominal value of its 'equity share capital' (issued share capital excluding any part which neither as respects dividend nor as respects capital carries any right to participate beyond a specified amount in a distribution), or
(c) it is a subsidiary of any company which is in turn a subsidiary of the holding company.

Group accounts must be presented as consolidated accounts unless the directors are of the opinion that another form would better serve the purpose (S. 151. 1948 Act). They must give a true and fair view of the state of affairs and profit or loss of the company and the subsidiaries dealt with by them as a whole, so far as concerns members of the holding company (S. 152. 1948 Act), the purpose of consolidated accounts being to present to the members of the holding company a statement regarding the group of companies as if they were a single undertaking.

Comment

828 The draft Fourth EEC Directive on Company law lays down detailed requirements for the contents of company accounts. As it is beyond the scope of this review to deal in detail with the present respective national requirements so is it beyond its scope to deal with the contents of the Directive.

Comparison

829 The absence of *compulsory* consolidated ('group') accounts in the Netherlands may make it more difficult than in England to assess the financial position of a group of companies as a whole, since the alternative of including subsidiaries' accounts in the explanatory notes to the holding company's accounts, without consolidating them, is permitted.

Furthermore, under Dutch law all participations of 15% or more must be stated with their full name and registered office in the accounts of the company holding the participation.

Alternatively a list of such participations may be deposited at the Trade Register's Office in which case reference to the existence of the list must be made in the accounts (Art. 14 WJ).

Similar provisions are known under English law. If an English company holds more than 10% of any class of the issued equity share capital of another company there must be included in its annual accounts, or attached to them, a statement of the name of that other company, the country of its incorporation, the class of shares in question, the percentage held, and the same information as regards any other class of shares held in that other company (S. 4 (1). 1967 Act). If a company holds such a number of shares in another company that the amount of them exceeds 10% of its own assets there must be included in its annual accounts, or attached to them, a statement of the name and country of incorporation of that other company and the identity and percentage held of any class of shares in that other company (S. 4 (2). 1967 Act).

PUBLICATION

Dutch law

830 It is in the requirements for publication of the company's accounts that the NV and the BV are dealt with differently. Each NV must deposit a copy of its annual accounts, together with the explanatory note, at the Trade Register's Office for public inspection. Deposit has to be made within eight days after the annual accounts are adopted (Art. 42c K). For the convenience of the shareholders, however, the directors are obliged to make the annual accounts and the explanatory note available for inspection at the company's office, from the day of the convocation of the general meeting in which the documents are to be discussed until the end of that meeting (Art. 42b K). Copies must be made available, free of charge, to shareholders and holders of Depositary Receipts on request.

831 The BV is in a different position. It, in general, is under no obligation to publish its annual accounts by means of deposit at the Trade Register's Office.

In a slightly adopted form it has to comply with the inspection period of at least fifteen days for shareholders at the company's office (Art. 57t K), taking into account that a BV can only issue *registered* Depositary Receipts. If, however, the BV conducts the business of banking or insurance, or if it has issued bearer debentures (or bearer certificates of registered debentures), the company has to deposit full accounts at the Trade Register's Office on the same basis as the NV (Art. 57u K). If a BV's total assets amount to Dfl. 8,000,000 or more and it employs at least 100 persons (including employees of Dutch subsidiary companies, more than 50% of the issued capital of which is held), deposit of the balance sheet and explanatory note, but not the profit and loss account, is required (Art. 57v K).

832 An exception to the rule is made in those cases where the BV's accounts are incorporated in the annual accounts of its parent company which has deposited such accounts at the Trade Register's Office, provided that (i) the parent company has accepted joint liability for the BV's contractual debts, or (ii) the BV conducts its business entirely outside the territory of the EEC (Artt. 57v and w K; Art. 38a WJ).

It should be noted that Art. 38a WJ not only applies to BV's but also to NV's. In all cases the parent company's declaration of joint liability has to be deposited at the Trade Register's Office. Such declaration may at any time be withdrawn at the parent company's discretion through deposit of another declaration to that effect. The withdrawal, however, has no effect on liabilities towards a creditor, incurred before the creditor could have learned of the withdrawal.

English law

833 Public and private companies must, with some exceptions, make a Return to the Registrar of Companies at least once in every calendar year i.e. January 1st to December 31st. This 'Annual Return' must give specified particulars relating to the company and must have annexed to it duly certified copies of every balance sheet, profit and loss account, auditor's report and directors' report laid before the GM during the period to which the Return relates. The White Paper contains a proposal that there should be an obligation specifically to file the annual accounts, and therefore, presumably, no longer merely as part of the Annual Return. It is also proposed that the accounts should be filed within a specified period after the end of the period to which they relate. It may be noted in passing that in the case of a private company there must also be annexed to the Annual Return certificates that it has not issued any invitation to the public to subscribe for its shares or debentures and, where the membership exceeds the statutory fifty, that the excess consists wholly of the permitted category of employees or ex-employees (See § 122 above).

Accordingly the requirement for filing with the Registrar and therefore availability for public inspection at the Registry applies equally to public and private companies. Furthermore, as explained in § 823 above, copies of the accounts and reports must be sent to members and debenture holders.

834 The fact that a subsidiary company's accounts may have been included in a consolidation with its parent company's accounts does not in any way diminish the obligation on the subsidiary company to produce its own accounts and reports, to send them to its shareholder(s) and to file them with the Registrar.

Comparison

835 The declaration of joint liability which, as set out above, a Dutch parent company may file with the Trade Register's Office in order to accept liability for the debts of its subsidiary, introduces a distinctive feature in the Dutch companies' 'Group-behaviour' which has no parallel in English law. It is sometimes contended, however, that the acceptance of joint liability constitutes a modification of the 'limited liability' characteristic of the subsidiary BV or NV in that the shareholder in the subsidiary accepts a liability in excess of its subscription of the shares it has taken in the subsidiary.

This might be called '*lifting the corporate veil*', a concept not generally known to Dutch Company law, but which is a known principle of English law.

836 It therefore seems appropriate to set out, briefly, the basis of this English principle of law.

As stated in § 138 above, all registered companies become legal entities in their own right with effect from the date of incorporation mentioned in the Certificate of Incorporation. It was also explained in § 212 above that if the number of members falls below the statutory minimum and the company continues to carry on business for more than six months, each member who is aware of the position becomes severally liable for all debts contracted after that period. This is one illustration of the law disregarding the principle of limited liability. There is a number of other instances in which this is done or the separate legal status of a company is disregarded:

(i) Under S. 332. of the 1948 Act, if in the course of winding-up it appears that any business of the company has been carried with intent to defraud creditors or for any fraudulent purpose, the Court may declare that any persons who were knowingly parties to it shall be personally responsible without any limitation of liability for such of the liabilities of the company as the Court directs.

(ii) There are many examples under tax legislation where corporate personality is disregarded, particularly in the case of private companies controlled by a limited number of persons. The object of these legislative provisions is to prevent persons obtaining tax advantages by incorporating themselves into a company which they would not otherwise enjoy. This subject is large and complicated and will not be dealt with further in this review.

However, it may be of interest to note that the place of registration of a company may be disregarded in determining its residence for tax purposes. The criterion for this is the place of the company's 'central management and control'.

(iii) In some cases the Courts have disregarded corporate personality where it acts as a cloak for fraud or improper conduct, for example where an individual formed a company to carry on a business and solicit customers of his former employer because he himself had agreed not to do so. An injunction was granted against the company although it had given no covenant itself.

837 It is felt, here, that although the declaration of joint liability under Dutch law bears a distinct resemblance, in principle, to the concept of lifting the corporate veil as known in English law, the concept cannot be generally accepted as a principle of Dutch law. Its application should therefore be strictly limited to those cases where statutory law provides for the phenomenon.

AUDITORS

Dutch law

838 The external audit of all NV's is obligatory and has to be carried out by a 'Register-accountant' (i.e. a member of the '*Nederlands Instituut voor Registeraccountants*')– BV's are generally exempt from this obligation, provided the BV neither has an issued capital of Dfl. 500,000 or more, nor is engaged in insurance or banking business, nor has issued bearer debentures (or bearer certificates of registered debentures), nor has an issued capital and reserves totalling Dfl. 8,000,000 or more and employs at the end of the financial year 100 employees or more (including, again, employees in 50% or more controlled subsidiaries).

Instead of by a Registeraccountant, the external audit may also be carried out by any 'foreign expert', who has obtained a (revocable) licence from the Minister of Economic Affairs on the basis of a certificate of capability acquired abroad (Artt. 42a and 57s K).

839 Except in those cases where Art. 38a WJ is applicable, the appointment of the auditor is made by the GM, which for that purpose cannot be restricted in its powers by any binding recommendation (Artt. 42a and 57s K). The board of 'Commissarissen' (if any) is also authorised to appoint the auditor, but the board can only exercise its powers if the GM did not make use of its right of appointment or did not–in a case where the appointment is obligatory–comply with the obligatory appointment (Artt. 51b and 58c K).

In all cases, where the appointment of a Registeraccountant is not compulsory, the GM or, alternatively, the board of 'Commissarissen' may appoint an 'expert'. The expert may be a Registeraccountant, but this is not compulsory (Art. 57s K).

English law

840 A company, whether public or private, must at each AGM appoint an auditor or auditors to hold office until the end of the next AGM but a retiring auditor is re-appointed without any resolution unless he is not qualified for the appointment, a Resolution has been passed to the contrary, or he has given the company notice in writing that he is not willing to be re-appointed. The directors are entitled to fill any casual vacancy in the office of auditor. If a Resolution is to be proposed contrary to the reappointment of the retiring auditor, the company must notify the retiring auditor who may require representations in writing to be notified to the shareholders.

While the first auditors of the company may be appointed by the directors before the first AGM, it will be seen that the GM can remove them and it is also entitled to appoint the first auditors if the directors do not do so (S. 159. 1948 Act).

841 In order to act as an auditor, a person must either be a member of a recognised body of accountants established in the United Kingdom or be authorised by the Department of Trade & Industry as having similar qualifications or adequate knowledge and experience. This applies to public and private companies alike, apart from some exemptions to cover auditors to a category of company which since the 1967 Act has otherwise become the same as the private company as described in this Review. Even if otherwise qualified for appointment as auditor, a person cannot be appointed if he is an officer or an employee of the company or a partner of or employed by such a person, a body corporate (*'juridische persoon'*) or disqualified by reason of any of the foregoing for appointment as auditor of a subsidiary or holding company of the company.

Comparison

842 It should be noted that English private companies must have a qualified auditor (or at least one recognised as competent) whereas some BV's are exempt from such a requirement, as explained above.

POSITION OF THE AUDITOR

Dutch law

843 The auditor is asked to audit the annual balance sheet, the profit and loss account and the explanatory notes, as drafted by the directors. To that end he is authorised to inspect all books and documents of the company, relevant to the proper exercise of his task. The auditor reports the results of his examinations to the GM. At the same time he informs the board of 'Commissarissen' of his findings. In practice, the GM receives a short report, whereas the 'Commissarissen' receive a detailed report, critically analysing the company's state of affairs (Artt. 42a and 57s K).

English law

844 The auditor's main duty is to make a report (the Auditor's Report) to the shareholders on the accounts examined by him and on the balance sheet, profit and loss account and group accounts (if any) laid before the GM. For this purpose he is entitled to access at all times to the books, accounts and records of the company and to require the officers of the company to give him such information and explanations as he thinks necessary for the performance of his duties. He is also entitled to attend *any* GM and to receive all notices of and communications relating to any GM (S. 14. 1967 Act).

Comparison

845 In the Netherlands the auditor has no automatic *right* to receive notice of or attend the GM at which the annual accounts are discussed. The practice however is developing for either the directors or the board of Commissarissen to *invite* the auditor to attend. This is still subject to approval at the GM in question. In England the auditor's right in this respect cannot be taken away by the directors or the GM.

PUBLICATION OF THE AUDITOR'S REPORT

Dutch law

846 The report, copies of which are available to shareholders, has to be deposited for inspection by the shareholders and interested third parties at the company's office together with the annual accounts and the explanatory note, as from the day of the convocation of the general meeting in which the annual accounts are to be discussed until the end of that meeting (Artt. 42b and 57t K). Once the annual accounts have been adopted and, as the case may be, approved by the GM it will be recalled that all relevant documents have to be filed, within eight days, with the Trade Register's Office. This requirement, of course, only applies to those companies who are obliged to publish their accounts. The documents have then to be accompanied by a statement of the Registeraccountant, setting out in brief the result of his audit. In practice, this statement is very short indeed and worded in standard form, telling the public–conditionally, if necessary–that the auditor approves the published documents since these, in his view, are drawn up in accordance with the reality of the company's financial state affairs.

English law

847 The Auditor's Report which, as mentioned in § 823 above has to be sent to shareholders and debenture holders with the accounts and has to be filed with the Registrar of Companies with the Annual Return, must include the following (S. 14 (3). 1967 Act):

1. A statement whether in the auditor's opinion the balance sheet and profit and loss account and group accounts (if any) have been properly prepared in accordance with the provisions of the Companies Acts.
2. A statement whether in the auditor's opinion the balance sheet gives a true and fair view of the state of the company's affairs at the end of its financial year.
3. A statement whether in the auditor's opinion the profit and loss account gives a true and fair view of the company's profit or loss for the financial year.

In the case of Group Accounts, the foregoing of course relates to the state of affairs and profit or loss of the company and its subsidiaries so far as concerns members of the company.

Unless the auditor has reason to qualify his Report, it is normally confined to the matters stated above and consequently short.

Comparison

848 Under English law there is no requirement of deposit of the auditor's report at the registered office, as it has to be sent to all shareholders together with the accounts and the directors' report.

EXPLANATORY NOTE AND DIRECTORS' REPORT

Dutch law

849 The explanatory note, which accompanies all accounts, has to set out the basic principles of valuation of the company's assets, which have been used in drawing up the accounts. Published accounts are, apart from the explanatory note, also accompanied by the annual report of directors in which their way of management of the company's business over the previous year is outlined and in which, not uncommonly, the directors give their view on the prospects of the company (Artt. 49 and 58c K). Although this is usually the case, there is no legal obligation for the directors to submit their report in writing.

Directors' Report

English law

850 As mentioned in § 823 above this must be attached to every balance sheet laid before the GM. Under the 1948 and 1967 Acts the following must be included in it:

1. Names of persons who were directors at any time during the year in question.
2. A report on the state of the company's affairs.
3. The principal activities of the company and its subsidiaries and significant changes during the year.
4. An explanation of any significant changes in the fixed assets of the company or its subsidiaries during the year.
5. Particulars of issues of shares or debentures during the year.
6. Particulars of any contracts of significance in which a director had a material interest.
7. Particulars of any arrangements enabling the directors to acquire benefits through the acquisition of shares or debentures of any body corporate, if the company is a party to those arrangements.
8. Any change in the interests of directors, their wives or husbands, or children under the age of 18 years, in shares or debentures of the company, its holding company or its subsidiaries.
9. The extent to which the turnover and profit or loss were attributable to different classes of business carried on by the company must be specified where the turnover exceeds £50,000 or in any case where the company is a holding or subsidiary company.
10. A statement of the average number of persons employed each week and their

aggregate remuneration. This does not apply if the number of employees is less than one hundred or the company is a wholly-owned subsidiary of a company incorporated in Great Britain.

11. Particulars of contributions for political or charitable purposes.
12. Particulars of the value of goods exported if the company's business includes the supplying of goods, and generally speaking the turnover exceeds £50,000, or it is a holding or subsidiary company.
13. The directors' proposals regarding dividend and any amount to be carried to reserves.

The White Paper indicates that the Government intends to extend the scope of information required in the Directors' Report, for example, to particulars of their service contracts, dealings in the company's shares, transactions by the company and other companies in which they have any significant interest, and possibly also the performance of the company in regard to the safety and health of its employees, the number of consumer complaints and how they were dealt with, the conduct of industrial relations, and a fuller disclosure of details of significant material acquisitions, realisations and contracts. It seems likely that this would apply only to public and large private companies.

Comparison

851 The fact that English law requires a written directors' report and lays down its contents in detail should be noted. The information given to shareholders is, consequently, greater in the case of an English company.

DIVIDEND

Dutch law

852 The basic rule, as laid down in Artt. 42d and 57r K, is that, unless otherwise provided in the Articles of Association, the profits are for the benefit of the shareholders. By virtue of the Ministerial Directives it is, however, possible to grant exclusive power to some body other than the GM to determine what amount of the positive outcome of the company's financial year–the company's profits as stated in the profit and loss account–will be added to the reserves, thus curtailing the GM's rights.

853 Although in principle all shareholders are to be treated equally departure from this rule is allowed to a certain extent (Artt. 39d and 57o K). The Articles of Association may restrict the rights of e.g. ordinary shareholders to the benefit of preference shareholders. Under no circumstances, however, is it allowed to exclude any shareholder from profit-sharing. It is permissible to provide, in the Articles of Association, that part of the profits will be distributed to others than shareholders (e.g. employees of the company). The Articles of Association must, in order to avoid any misunderstanding, contain detailed rules as to who these 'others' are and in what way the profits will be shared between them and the shareholders. Such matters may not be decided at the discretion of any body of the company.

854 Dividend may be claimed by individual shareholders for a period of five years after having been declared, unless a longer time limit has expressly been provided for (Artt. 42d and 57r K).

English law

855 A company is not bound to distribute profits to shareholders as dividends in the absence of a provision in the company's Articles of Association requiring this to be done. The directors have a discretion as to what part, if any, of the profits should be distributed as dividend and what part (if any) should be carried to reserve.

Without the declaration or the recommendation of the directors a shareholder is not, therefore, generally entitled to require distribution of profits.

856 The Articles of Association normally stipulate the proportion in which profits which it is decided to distribute should be divided between the shareholders. This is usually in accordance with the amount paid or credited as paid on their shares (e.g. Regulation 118 of Table A). Different classes of shares may be entitled only to dividends of restricted amount either in priority to or after payment of dividend to other shareholders.

857 There is no provision in the Companies Acts as to who should declare a dividend and therefore the Articles of Association may give this power to the directors. Normally, however, the directors are empowered to pay interim dividends from time to time but the final dividend may be declared by the company in GM up to a maximum of the amount recommended by the directors.

Once a dividend has been declared and has become payable it is a debt for which a shareholder can sue and in England a shareholder has twelve years in which to recover it.

Comparison

858 The principal difference is that the shareholders of a Dutch company are entitled to influence the way in which profits are dealt with since, unless the Articles provide otherwise, profits are in principle for the benefit of shareholders. The English approach is the exact opposite.

IX. Investigation into a company's affairs

Dutch law

901 Until 1971 a limited form of investigation into a company's affairs was known in the form of an inquiry on the initiative of holders of at least one-fifth of the issued capital. This right of inquiry was restricted to NV's only. (It was not applicable to other forms of undertakings and it will be recalled that, in any case, the BV did not exist at the time.) The legal requirements were not compulsory for the then existing small family-NV's with a few registered shares. The effect of an inquiry could only be of a preventative nature, because no measures could be ordered by the Court, and a majority of shareholders in most cases still formed too large a block for the inquiring minority to bring about those changes, which the outcome of the investigation suggested to be necessary.

902 With the new provisions contained in the 1971 Right of Inquiry Act, investigations into a company's affairs are regulated in a more meaningful and, certainly, more extended way.

903 The rules for an inquiry are laid down in Artt. 53–54d K and apply equally to NV's and BV's (Art. 58c K). The procedure may now be summarised as follows:

(a) A request for an inquiry may be made to the Commercial Chamber of the Amsterdam Court of Appeal by various (groups of) persons (Art. 53 K) i.e.:

- shareholders, representing at least one tenth of the issued capital;
- holders of Depositary Receipts, which represent a nominal countervalue of Dfl. 500,000 or any less amount as specified in the Articles of Association;
- an Association of Workers, members of which are employed in the relevant company. This Association must have possessed legal personality for more than two years, and its bye-laws must mention as one of the objects the safeguarding of the interests of its members. Apart from these requirements the Association has to have played an active part in the company concerned or in the branch of economic activity in which the company is engaged. It can only file the request if it has taken advice from the Works Council (if any) of the company concerned;
- any other persons, who have the right to demand an inquiry by virtue of the Articles of Association or by agreement with the company;
- The Attorney-General of the Amsterdam Court of Appeal (for reasons of public interest).

(b) If the Commercial Chamber is of the opinion that the request is justified it appoints one or more investigators. The inquiry may be directed at certain aspects of the company's policy or at the whole of its affairs (Art. 53 K).
(c) Before a decision is reached, all interested parties, including the company's directors and board of 'Commissarissen' (if any), are heard. The Commercial Chamber may also hear experts before deciding (Artt. 53–53a K).
(d) The investigators are entitled to full access to all the company's books, accounts and other records and must be admitted to the company's premises. Directors, 'Commissarissen' and, in general, all employees must co-operate in the investigation, if requested. The investigators may even seek a Court Order for access to the books, accounts and other records of other companies, provided these have been, or are, closely connected with the company to be investigated (Art. 53b K).
(e) The outcome of the investigation has to be filed with the Clerk of the Court of Appeal of Amsterdam. The petitioner(s), the Attorney-General and the company receive a copy of the report. The Commercial Chamber may decide that the report will be open for public inspection, in which case an announcement has to be made in the Official Gazette (Art. 53d K).
(f) Depending on the outcome of the investigation the costs of it may, by request of the company, be allocated to the petitioner(s), or to one or more directors or 'Commissarissen' personally if it has become clear that he or they have been to blame for mismanagement of the company (Art. 53e K).
(g) If the report shows reasons to believe that the company has been mismanaged, the Commercial Chamber may impose measures to improve the situation. A request to that end has to be filed with the Commercial Chamber, within two months after the deposit of the report, by any of those entitled to ask for an inquiry (Art. 54 K): Measures possible in this context are laid down exhaustively in Art. 54 K:

- suspension or reversal of a Resolution passed by any body of the company;
- suspension or removal of one or more directors or 'Commissarissen';
- temporary appointment of one or more directors or 'Commissarissen';
- temporary departure from certain provisions of the Articles of Association, as indicated by the Commercial Chamber;
- 'dissolution' of the company (see for terminology § 1101 below).

(h) The Commercial Chamber indicates the period of validity of any temporary measure and regulates, if necessary, the consequences of any measures (Art. 54b K).
(j) Decisions taken by the Commercial Chamber may take immediate effect upon the Chamber's order (Art. 54c K). The company and those entitled to ask for an inquiry have the right to appeal ('*cassatie*') to the Supreme Court of the Netherlands ('*Hoge Raad der Nederlanden*') against any of the Commercial Chamber's decisions under the foregoing (Art. 54d K).

Inspection of a Company's books and papers

English law

904 Under S. 109 of the 1967 Act, the Department of Trade & Industry has power to require any public or private company to produce such books or papers as it may require, provided that the Department is satisfied that there is good reason to do so. This power enables the Department to inspect the books and papers of any company.

Investigation into the affairs of a company, the ownership of its shares, or dealings in its shares or debentures

905 The Department of Trade & Industry has power in certain circumstances to carry out investigation into the above matters. The Department may investigate the ownership of shares on its own but the other investigations must be carried out by an inspector or inspectors appointed by the Department.

Under S. 164 of the 1948 Act the Department has power to appoint inspectors to investigate the affairs of a company if either not less than 200 members or members holding not less than one-tenth of the issued shares so request. The Department is not bound to take any action on such a request.

906 Under S. 165 of the 1948 Act, the Department is *obliged* to appoint inspectors to investigate the affairs of a company if either the company by Special Resolution of the GM or the Court by Order, declares that the company's affairs ought so to be investigated. Under the same Section the Department has power, *but is not obliged,* to appoint inspectors to investigate a company's affairs if it appears to the Department that there are circumstances suggesting:

(i) that its business is being conducted with intent to defraud creditors, whether of itself or of any other person;
(ii) that its business is being conducted for any other fraudulent or unlawful purpose or in a manner oppressive of any part of its members;
(iii) that it was formed for any fraudulent or unlawful purpose;
(iv) that persons concerned with its formation or the management of its affairs have, in that connection, been guilty of fraud or other misconduct towards the company or its members; or
(v) that its members have not been given all the information with respect to its affairs which they might reasonably expect.

An inspector appointed under the foregoing provisions may if he thinks it necessary also investigate the affairs of any holding or subsidiary company of the company.

Except where the Department is obliged to carry out an investigation, it does not often do so since, generally speaking, shareholders are expected to rely upon their rights under the company's Memorandum and Articles of Association.

907 Inspectors appointed by the Department must at the end of their investigation make a report to the Department and the Department must send a copy to the registered office of the company; if it thinks fit, to any member of the company or any creditor whose interests appear to the Board to be affected; to the applicants for the investigation where it is carried out pursuant to S. 164 of the 1948 Act; and to the Court where the investigation is pursuant to S. 165 of the 1948 Act. The Department may also cause the report to be printed and published (S. 168. 1948 Act).

If, from the report, it appears to the Department that any criminal offence has been committed, the matter may be referred to the Director of Public Prosecutions who may institute proceedings accordingly. If, from the report, it appears to the Department expedient to do so by reason of any of the circumstances mentioned in the previous paragraph in relation to S. 165 of the 1948 Act, the Department may present a petition for the company to be wound up on the 'just and equitable' ground (see § 1115 below) or for an Order under S. 210 of the 1948 Act (oppression of minorities, as to which see in § 631 above) or both (S. 35. 1967 Act).

The Department also has power to bring civil proceedings on behalf of the company to recover damages for any fraud or other misconduct in connection with its promotion, formation or management of its affairs or the recovery of any property which has been misapplied or wrongfully retained.

Investigation into membership

908 The Department of Trade & Industry, where it appears that there is good reason to do so, *may* appoint inspectors to investigate and report on the membership of any company for the purpose of determining the true persons who are or have been financially interested in its success or failure or able to control or materially influence its policies. The Department *is under an obligation to do so* with respect to particular shares or to debentures of a company if so requested by members of the company who in number or by proportion of issued shares held would qualify under S. 164 of the 1948 Act (see § 905 above).

The Department may even in these circumstances decline to do so if they are satisfied that the application is vexatious (S. 172. 1948 Act). As indicated above, the Department may also investigate the ownership of shares or debentures without appointing an inspector. In either case, if a person causes difficulty by unwillingness to assist an investigation, the Department may make an order restricting the exercise of rights attached to the shares in question.

Investigation of dealings in shares or debentures

909 Under S. 32 of the 1967 Act, if it appears to the Department of Trade & Industry that there are circumstances suggesting that there may have been contraventions of the provisions of that Act concerning the prohibition of dealings by directors in options over listed shares or debentures of that company (S. 25. 1967 Act), of the obligation of a director to notify a company of his interests in shares or debentures of the company or associated companies (S. 27. 1967 Act, and see § 850 above) or the obligation of a director to notify a company or the grant or exercise by his wife or her husband or his or her sons or daughters under the age of eighteen years of a right to subscribe for shares or debentures in the company (S. 31. 1967 Act) the Department *may* appoint inspectors to investigate.

Comparison

910 Although investigations into the affairs of a Dutch company are supervised by a judicial body instead of by a Government Department as in England, the proceedings in the two countries bear much similarity. The powers of the inspectors seem to be equivalent and the measures which may be taken are of the same tenor.

However, it should be noted that both systems have aspects not known in the other.

911 To start with English investigations; these may be initiated by 200 or more members in a company, which means that, especially in listed companies, a much smaller percentage than the alternatively required holders of 10% of the issued shares may call for an investigation. This system seems more flexible than the simple 10% requirement under Dutch law.

Another difference from Dutch law is the power of the Department of Trade & Industry to carry out investigations on its own initiative, wherever it thinks that there is a good reason to do so. It is felt that this goes further than the Dutch system where the investigation may be requested by the Attorney-General of the Amsterdam Court of Appeal for reasons of public interest. Finally, it is also thought that the Department's power to appoint inspectors to investigate dealings in shares or debentures is already one step further down the road of ousting 'insider dealings' (see §§ 1240–1241 below), since in the Netherlands no statutory provisions in that respect exist as yet.

912 The Dutch provisions on the other hand provide for safeguards for the employees in a company through the granting of the right to request an investigation to an association of workers. This right is consistent with the existence of Works Councils with a strong influence in the running of the company's business. Under the present situation in England workers' organisations are only likely to bring about an investigation if they can put enough pressure on the Department of Trade & Industry for it to start an investigation on its own initiative.

X. Amendment of Constitution Documents

Dutch law

1001 The rules relating to the amendment of a NV's Articles of Association are laid down in Artt. 45–45f K. These articles apply accordingly to the amendment of a BV's Articles by virtue of Art. 58b K.

1002 In principle it is the GM which has the power to decide upon amendment by a simple majority. This power cannot be taken away from it in order to grant it to other bodies of the company, but it may be restricted by 'oligarchic' clauses (e.g. requiring a 3/4 majority or the prior approval of a meeting of holders of priority shares). The power may, however, be taken away altogether. In all cases where the GM's normal power is restricted or excluded, the GM may nevertheless override and change any 'oligarchic' clause of that kind in the Articles of Association by unanimous vote in a meeting at which the entire issued capital is represented (Art. 45 K), or by a decision taken in accordance with the terms of the restriction.

1003 Usually the directors are granted the right to make any proposals for amendment. Such proposals, in the case of 'large' companies (Artt. 52n and 58c K) have to be approved by the board of 'Commissarissen'. If the directors propose amending the Articles of Association, all shareholders must be given ample opportunity to consider the proposals. Not only (and despite Art. 43g K) should the directors summarise the proposed changes in the notice convening the meeting at which they are to be decided upon, but the directors, or those who convene the meeting must also deposit a full text of the proposed amendments at the company's office from the day of convening the meeting, until the end of the meeting. In this way inspection by the shareholders is made possible. Free copies of the proposals must be made available to shareholders on request (Art. 45b K). It should be noted that the safeguards of the interests of the shareholders apply equally to holders of Depositary Receipts which are issued with the co-operation of the company.

1004 The amendments must be set out in a notarial deed and, prior to their coming into effect, the Ministerial declaration of non-objection must be obtained. Before issuing the declaration, the Ministry checks whether the resolution to amend the Articles has been passed in accordance with the law and the provisions in the existing Articles. The declaration may be refused for the same reasons as apply in the case of the deed of incorporation (Art. 45d K).

It is laid down in Art. 45d K that no change of Articles can take away the rights of persons other than shareholders. Furthermore no amendment of the Articles can be effected without the consent of the Receiver during the company's bankruptcy.

Alteration of Memorandum of Association

English law

1005 Except to the extent authorised by the 1948 Act, the Memorandum of Association cannot be altered. As to permissible alterations, a distinction must be made between the compulsory clauses (listed in § 203 above) and any additional clauses which need not have been contained in the Memorandum of Association anyway.

The following compulsory clauses can be altered in the manner stated below:

1. *The Name Clause:* By Special Resolution, but with the approval of the Department of Trade & Industry to the new name (S. 18. 1948 Act).
2. *The Objects Clause:* By Special Resolution, but only in order to enable the company to do one or more of seven specified things. A specified minority of shareholders or of certain debenture holders may apply to the Court within twenty- one days after the passing of the resolution, for the alteration to be cancelled. If such application is made, the alteration only has effect so far as confirmed by the Court. If no application is made, the validity of the alteration cannot subsequently be questioned even on the ground that it did not fall within one of the seven specified things. In most cases therefore, the seven specified things are of little importance and therefore has been omitted from this Review. (They are set out in S. 5 (1). 1948 Act.)
3. *The Capital Clause:* The procedure specified in §§ 816 and 820 above for increase and reduction of capital respectively must be followed.

Any additional clauses in the Memorandum can be altered in the same manner as the Objects of the company and subject to the same right of objection, unless the Memorandum prohibits the alteration or itself provides a procedure for the alteration. Alteration of such additional clauses may also amount to a variation of the class rights of a Class of Members in which case the procedure referred to in § 305 above must also be followed.

Alteration of Articles of Association

1006 Under S. 10 of the 1948 Act a company may by Special Resolution alter or add to its Articles, but subject to any conditions in its Memorandum. There are two ways in which this power conferred by the Act may be limited so far as the alteration of a particular Article is concerned. One is for a special class of shares to be issued, one of the rights attached to which is to veto any alteration of the Article. The other is for the Article to provide that the shares held by a specified person will carry over twenty-five per cent of all the votes which can be cast upon any Resolution to alter the Article. As a Special Resolution requires a seventy-five per cent majority, this can be effective to prevent the alteration. Apart from these special cases, the provisions of the Section are subject to the general considerations against fraud on a minority of shareholders or violation of any legal principles.

If a company contracts with a third party not to alter its Articles, this will be ineffective. Alteration in such circumstances may, however, amount to a breach of contract giving rise to a liability to pay compensation.

Comparison

1007 The procedure in Dutch and English law appears to be very similar except (i) that the Ministerial declaration of non-objection is required for any alteration in the Netherlands, however insignificant, whereas official control is only in practice exercised in England as regards change of name; (ii) that, arising out of the existence of the separate Memorandum and Articles of Association for English companies, shareholders may object to alterations of certain clauses in the Memorandum even if approved by the requisite majority; and (iii), apart from changes of capital, a 75% majority is required in English law for alteration of the Memorandum and Articles of Association, compared with the absolute majority in Dutch law in the absence of higher requirements in the Articles of Association.

XI. Winding-up

Dutch law

1101 The 'dissolution' ('*ontbinding*') of a Dutch company on one of the grounds mentioned below means–as contrasted with the English terminology–that the relationship between the shareholders, required for the company's existence, has been disturbed. The result is that the company's winding-up ('*vereffening*') has to take place. The 'dissolved' company only comes to an end when the winding-up by the liquidators has been completed.

Grounds for 'dissolution'

1102 Dutch Company law indicates exhaustively grounds on which companies can be 'dissolved' and all material provisions regulating the cause of action after the 'dissolution' are equally applicable to NV's and BV's (Art. 58g K). Grounds for 'dissolution' are:

(i) As stated in the Articles of Association (Artt. 55 and 58d K);
(ii) By resolution to that effect passed by the GM (Artt. 55 and 58d K);
(iii) By its insolvency after the company has been declared bankrupt or by termination of the bankruptcy because of the–hopeless–situation of the estate (Artt. 55 and 58d K);
(iv) By order of the Court. This may occur in the following cases;
  (a) The deed of incorporation is defective.
  This is so if the notarial deed lacks the force of an 'authentic' deed–this is the technical Dutch term for a notarised deed–or if the incorporation was not done by two or more incorporators, all of whom also participated in the initial capital issued (Art. 36j K);
  (b) The Public Prosecutor may demand the 'dissolution' if he is of the opinion that the company's object or activity is contrary to public morality or public order (Art. 37b K);
  (c) The Commercial Chamber of the Court of Appeal of Amsterdam may declare the company 'dissolved' if after an inquiry within the meaning of Art. 53 K it is found that the company has been grossly mismanaged (Artt. 54–54a K). This power to make an order is subject to the restriction that the 'dissolution' must not be contrary to the interest of the company's shareholders or employees, nor to the public interest (Art. 54b K). Details of the inquiry procedure are set out above in Chapter IX.

In all cases mentioned under (a)–(c) the dissolution takes effect upon the Court order becoming final.

1103 In the case of Art. 36j K the 'dissolution' will be published in the Official Gazette for which publication the Clerk of the Court is responsible. Art. 37b K requires public registration, by the Court-appointed Receiver, of the 'dissolution' at the Trade Register's Office. The decision of the Commercial Chamber under Art. 54 K will be deposited at the Trade Register's Office by the Clerk of the Court of Appeal (Art. 54c K).

1104 One of the grounds for 'dissolution' originating in the Articles of Association may be the fact that the company was only formed for a limited period of time. If that period has expired without extension of the term through a timely amendment of the Articles of Association the term is nevertheless automatically extended by one year, if:

(i) before expiration of the limited period, the GM has passed a resolution to extend it;
(ii) a copy of this resolution has at the same time (i.e. before expiration of the limited period) been deposited at the Trade Register's Office;
(iii) an announcement to draw the attention of the public to the proposed extension is made in the Official Gazette and one of the local newspapers of the place where the company's registered office is situated (Art. 55a K).

Publication

1105 The general rule is that knowledge of the 'dissolution' of the company has to be available to the public through publication in the Official Gazette and through deposit of a statement of 'dissolution' at the Trade Register's Office (Art. 55b K). Apart from publication the company has to indicate on all printed matter it sends out that it is in liquidation by adding the word '*in liquidatie*' (meaning 'in liquidation') to the company's name.

Liquidation

1106 The result of the company's 'dissolution' is that it has to be liquidated. For the purposes of liquidation the company remains in existence as a legal entity but all its activities have to be directed towards the winding-up of its property (Art. 55c K).

Unless the Articles of Association provide otherwise the directors of the company will act as its liquidators (Art. 55d K).

The provisions relating to appointment, suspension and dismissal of directors apply accordingly to these liquidators. If the power to appoint liquidators is vested in the GM it may appoint any appropriate person.

In contrast to the general rules set out in this paragraph a Receiver will be appointed by the Court in case of 'dissolution' under Art. 37b K. Such a Receiver will then be responsible for the winding-up of the company pursuant to the provisions of the

Bankruptcy Act (*'Faillissementswet'*). By virtue of Art. 54d K the Commercial Chamber of the Court of Appeal of Amsterdam has the right to take any appropriate measures in respect of the appointment of liquidators, if it considers this necessary.

The last exception to the rule applies if the company is declared bankrupt. Such declaration is issued by the Bankruptcy Chamber of the competent District Court and has to be accompanied by the appointment of an independent Receiver, who has the duty of winding-up the company's assets under the supervision of a Judge in accordance with the provisions of the Bankruptcy Act.

Liquidation balance

1107 Whatever money is left over after the creditors have been paid out of the proceeds of the company's assets will be distributed among the shareholders in proportion to their holdings. It should be noted that the fact of the company's 'dissolution' does not cause the creditors to lose any rights. Although it is remarkable that Dutch Company law contains no provision whatsoever for the compulsory public convocation of creditors, except for the publication requirements, in order to draw their attention to the liquidation or to invite them to submit their claims, the individual creditor has the right to safeguard his position e.g. by seizing (part of) the company's assets or seeking the company's bankruptcy. Once the bankruptcy has been declared the Receiver is under an obligation to announce the bankruptcy publicly and to send a circular to all known creditors in order to invite them to submit their claims.

1108 The law also contains provisions for a plan of distribution of assets and the methods of opposing such a plan (Art. 56a K), the possibility of an interim distribution with the consent of the Court (Art. 56b K), the rendering of account by the liquidators (Art. 56e K) and the custody of the company's business records by any person designated by the Articles of Association or as appointed by the GM, if the Articles do not contain such a designation (Art. 56h K).

Completion of the liquidation

1109 The liquidation is considered to be completed once the liquidators have distributed the 'balance of the liquidation' to those persons entitled to it. It is then that the 'dissolved' company comes to an end, although under certain circumstances the liquidation may be re-opened by Court Order (Art. 56f K).

English law

1110 Apart from a power given to the Registrar, after he has given due notice, to remove a company from the Register on the grounds that it is neither carrying on business nor in operation (S. 353. 1948 Act) the only way in which the existence of a registered company can be ended is through the process of winding-up. Winding-up can take the following forms:

(i) *Compulsory* (i.e. by the Court).
(ii) *Voluntary*, which may be either under the supervision of the Court or without the supervision of the Court. Voluntary winding-up without Court supervision may further be either a Members' voluntary winding-up or a Creditors' voluntary winding-up.

Voluntary Winding-up

1111 Under S. 278 of the 1948 Act a company may be wound up voluntarily:

(a) On the expiration of a period fixed for its duration or the occurrence of an event specified in the Articles to cause dissolution. In this case winding-up may be commenced by an Ordinary Resolution of the GM, or
(b) If a Special Resolution of the GM is passed to wind the company up voluntarily, or
(c) If an Extraordinary Resolution of the GM is passed to the effect that the company cannot by reason of its liabilities continue its business and that it is advisable to wind up.

Under S. 280 of the 1948 Act a voluntary winding-up commences when the Resolution is passed. The Resolution must be advertised within fourteen days in the London Gazette (S. 279. 1948 Act). On commencement of the winding-up the company must cease to carry on its business except so far as required for the beneficial winding-up of it but the corporate status and powers of the company continue until it is dissolved (S. 281. 1948 Act). As explained further below, dissolution, i.e. the end of the existence of the company, does not take place until after the end of the winding-up.

1112 Under S. 285 of the 1948 Act, the GM must appoint one or more liquidators for the purpose of winding-up the affairs and distributing the assets of the company and may fix the remuneration to be paid to them. On appointment, all powers of the directors cease, except so far as the GM or the liquidator approves their continuation (S. 285. 1948 Act).

1113 If a majority of the directors make and file a formal declaration that they have made a full enquiry into the affairs of the company and as a result are of the opinion that the company will be able to pay its debts in full within a period not exceeding twelve months from the commencement of the winding-up, the winding-up will be a Members' voluntary winding-up. The declaration must have been made within the five weeks up to the winding-up resolution and must contain a statement of assets and liabilities as at the latest practicable date. There are penalties for making such a declaration without reasonable grounds and the burden of proof, contrary to the normal principle of criminal law, is on the accused director (S. 283. 1948 Act). The winding-up is a Creditors' voluntary winding-up if such declaration is not made or if, although it has been made, the liquidator is of the opinion that the company will not be able to pay

its debts in full within the stated period. A meeting of creditors must in this case be held. Notice must be given to creditors of the meeting and it must also be advertised in the London Gazette and in two local newspapers circulating in the district where the registered office or principal place of business is situated (S. 293. 1948 Act).

1114 A statement of the assets and liabilities of the company must be laid before the Creditors' Meeting and the creditors may nominate a liquidator. This nomination will take precedence over any nomination by the GM. The Creditors' Meeting may also appoint a 'Committee of Inspection' to represent the creditors and the company is entitled to appoint up to five persons to be members of this committee.

The Liquidator must summon a GM and a Creditors' Meeting at the end of the first and each following year and lay an account of the winding-up before them (S. 299. 1948 Act). As soon as the company's affairs are fully wound up the Liquidator must make up a final account and call a GM and a Creditors' Meeting for the purpose of laying the accounts before them. Such meetings are called by advertisement in the London Gazette. Within one week after the meeting the Liquidator must make a Return to the Registrar of Companies with a copy of the account. The Registrar then registers the Return and the account and three months after such registration the company is deemed to be dissolved unless in the meantime any interested person obtains a Court Order to defer the dissolution.

Winding-up by the Court ('Compulsory Winding-up')

1115 A company *may* be wound up by the Court if (S. 222. 1948 Act):

(a) The GM has passed a Special Resolution to that effect;
(b) Default is made in delivering the statutory report to the Registrar or in holding the statutory meeting (this applies only to a company incorporated as a public company and is therefore rare–see § 314 above);
(c) The company does not commence business within a year of incorporation or suspends its business for a whole year;
(d) The number of members is reduced below the statutory minimum (Private Company: 2, Public Company: 7);
(e) The company is unable to pay its debts (this is a technical expression defined in S. 223 of the 1948 Act);
(f) The Court is of the opinion that it is just and equitable that the company should be wound up.

1116 The winding-up by the Court is sought by way of petition which may be presented by the company, a creditor, a contributory (see below), by the Official Receiver (where a voluntary or supervised winding-up cannot be continued with due regard to the interests of the creditors or contributories), or by the Department of Trade & Industry where in consequence of an investigation it appears expedient in the public interest (S. 224. 1948 Act and S. 35. 1967 Act).

The petition must be advertised, seven clear days before the hearing, in the London Gazette and a local newspaper and must be served on the company. If the Court makes a winding-up Order, the winding-up dates from the presentation of the petition to the Court except where it is made after a voluntary winding-up, when it dates from the passing of the Resolution for winding-up (SS. 229 and 280. 1948 Act).

Unless the Court directs otherwise, the Order makes void any disposals of property made since the presentation of the petition (S. 227. 1948 Act), terminates the employment of employees and agents of the company, and dismisses and terminates the powers of the directors. Business documents after the winding-up Order must contain a statement that the company is in liquidation (S. 338. 1948 Act).

A copy of the winding-up Order is delivered to the Registrar of Companies and the Official Receiver is notified (S. 230. 1948 Act). The Official Receiver acts as provisional Liquidator and calls on the directors to supply a statement of the company's affairs on oath. He must summon meetings of the creditors and contributories to decide whether the Court should be asked to appoint a Liquidator in his place. If the Court does not do so, the Official Receiver is the Liquidator (S. 239. 1948 Act). Apart from determining whether an application should be made to the Court to appoint a liquidator in place of the Official Receiver, the business of the first meetings of the creditors and contributories is to determine whether or not the Court should be asked to appoint a Committee of Inspection. This, apart from one exceptional case applying only in Scotland, consists of creditors and contributories of the company.

1117 The duties and powers of the Liquidator are laid down in the 1948 Act and, in general, consist of protecting the assets and drawing up lists of contributories and creditors, realising assets under the control of the Committee of Inspection if there is one, paying the company's debts, and dividing any surplus amongst the contributories.

It should be noted that a 'contributory' is any person liable to contribute to the assets of the company in the event of it being wound up. These include all present members and past members who ceased to be members within one year before the commencement of the winding-up. In any event, a contributory cannot be required to contribute any greater amount than that for the time being unpaid on his shares and a past member is not liable in respect of any debt of the company incurred after he ceased to be a member (SS. 212–3. 1948 Act).

1118 In a compulsory winding-up creditors must 'prove' their debts or claims. This is done by submission of a verification on oath.

Under S. 256 of the 1948 Act a Court may on application being made to it stay the winding-up proceedings if it thinks fit.

When the affairs of the company have been completely wound up the Court, on the application of the Liquidator, makes an Order that the company be dissolved from the date of the Order. This Order must be forwarded to the Registrar of Companies within fourteen days for registration (S. 274. 1948 Act).

Winding-up under Supervision of the Court

1119 As explained above, this is a type of voluntary winding-up and is effected by Court Order made after the passing of the voluntary winding-up Resolution. It is not commonly used but has some advantages such as the fact that the Court may appoint an additional Liquidator and require more frequent reports on progress of the winding-up than would otherwise be the case and that the Order has the same effect as a winding-up Order in suspending other proceedings against the company.

Comparison
1120 In both systems, winding-up does not have to be, but may be, supervised by the Court.

In English law known creditors must be notified and there must also be official and local advertisement of the winding-up in all cases where the directors do not formally declare the solvency of the company. Although this system is open to abuse by directors prepared to risk criminal sanctions, it is, at least in theory, more favourable to creditors than the Dutch system involving only official advertisement and registration.

Attention is drawn again to the differences in terminology namely that 'dissolution' in English law is used to refer to the termination of the existence of the company *after* the liquidation or winding-up process whereas in Dutch law it is used to refer to the *commencement* of the liquidation process. In English law this is usually referred to as 'the commencement of the winding-up'.

RECONSTRUCTIONS AND ARRANGEMENTS

Dutch law
1121 No equivalent provisions.

Reconstructions

English law
1122 If a company desires to rearrange its capital structure in a way which would require the consent of all shareholders but some shareholders cannot be contacted or may not agree to the rearrangement, two methods are provided under the 1948 Act.

Under S. 287 of that Act where a company is being wound-up voluntarily or it is proposed that ('the first company') it should be wound-up voluntarily, and it is proposed that the whole or part of its business should be transferred or sold to another company ('the second company'), the liquidator of the first company may with the approval of a Special Resolution of the first company receive in compensation for the transfer or sale shares, policies, or like interests in the second company for distribution to the members of the first company or may enter into an arrangement under which the members of the first company will participate in the profits of or receive other benefits from the second company. Accordingly three-quarters of the members attending and voting at an EGM of the first company may bind all the members of the first company. A dissenting member may require the Liquidator either to abstain from carrying the Resolution into effect or to purchase his interest in the first company at a price to be determined by agreement or arbitration.

1123 It will be noted that this Section does not apply to a compulsory liquidation but a similar procedure is in that case available under S. 245 of the 1948 Act. Approval of the Court or the Committee of Inspection is necessary for the use of S. 287 if the winding-up is a *creditors'* voluntary winding-up.

The Section, although apparently included in the 1948 Act to facilitate the work of liquidators, can be used, inter alia, for the purpose of amalgamating two companies by the transfer of the business of one to the other, or for the purpose of amalgamating two companies by transferring the businesses of both to a new third company in exchange for shares in the third company which are issued to the shareholders of the first two companies in exchange for their shares in those companies.

A scheme of reconstruction under S. 287 may be challenged either by an action by shareholders against the company or by the making, within a year after the passing of the Special Resolution, of an Order by the Court for winding-up the company by it or under its supervision. In the latter case the Special Resolution is not valid unless approved by the Court.

Arrangements

1124 Under S. 206 of the 1948 Act, the Court has power to order meetings of creditors or members, or classes of either, to be summoned for the purpose of considering a compromise or arrangement proposed between a company and its creditors or members of any class of either. At such a meeting a 50% majority of those present and voting in person or by proxy can bind all creditors or members or relevant classes of them provided that the majority represents at least three-quarters in value of the creditors, members or class and the compromise or arrangement is approved by the Court.

The meetings may be summoned by notice sent to creditors or members or by advertisement or both as the Court directs, and in every notice or advertisement there must be included a statement explaining the effect of the compromise or arrangement and any material interest of the directors or the company in it.

1125 Under S. 208 of the 1948 Act, where a compromise or arrangement under S. 206 is proposed in connection with a scheme for the reconstruction of any company or the amalgamation of two or more companies and the whole or any part of the undertaking or property of any company involved is to be transferred to another company, the Court has wide powers to facilitate the reconstruction or amalgamation. For example, it may order the transfer from one company to another of the whole or part of its undertaking, property, or liabilities, the allotting to or appropriation by one company of any shares, debentures or policies, the dissolution without winding-up of any company which transfers its undertaking or property under the scheme, and provision for dissentients.

Therefore, while S. 206 may primarily have been intended to enable a company in financial difficulties to come to a compromise with its creditors, the scope of that Section, particularly as extended by S. 208 is much greater. In the event S. 206 has been extensively used by companies to effect mergers and reorganisations, particularly in circumstances when the provisions for compulsory acquisition of shares in S. 209 mentioned below are inapplicable.

Under S. 209 of the 1948 Act there is power to acquire compulsorily shares of a dissentient minority where a scheme or contract involving transfer of shares or any class of shares has been approved by the holders of not less than nine-tenths in value of the shares in question (excluding shares already held by the transferee company or any subsidiary of it). However, the most common use of S. 209 is in connection with take-over bids and it is therefore dealt with in § 1239 below.

Comment

1126 There are no provisions under Dutch law relating to reconstructions and arrangements.

The draft Third EEC Directive, however, requires in Art. 20 that the Member States lay down rules on transactions by means of which a company transfers the whole of its assets, as a result of *dissolution without liquidation*, to another company which holds all the shares of the acquired company.

It is therefore noteworthy that provisions at least comparable to those of SS. 206 and 208 of the 1948 Act will have to be implemented in due course.

XII. Take-over Codes

Dutch law

SER–Besluit Fusiegedragsregels 1971

1201 As stated in § 106 above the SER has issued rules in respect of mergers and take-overs, which have two main purposes: the protection of shareholders and the protection of employees. Another aspect dealt with in the Code–albeit still in an experimental and very preliminary way–is the notification of take-overs falling within the rules of the Code to the Government, i.e. the Minister of Economic Affairs. The provisions relating to this underline the development of the idea of the desirability of the Government having some form of control over those take-overs which might lead to any unwanted dominant position in the country.

The Code is divided into four chapters and contains merely procedural provisions. It is not concerned with the commercial merits of proposed take-overs.

1202 *Chapter I* deals with definitions and the protection of the shareholders' interests.

It is clear that the Code, although applicable to both NV's and BV's only relates to 'public offers', i.e. a public announcement by a company (regardless of its nationality) containing either an invitation to make an offer to sell or to buy shares in a company which are listed on the Amsterdam Stock Exchange or in which a regular trade exists in any other way. It is noteworthy that wherever the Code speaks of shares it also envisages Depositary Receipts.

The Code in this chapter only speaks of 'public offers' thus avoiding the words 'merger' ('*fusie*') or 'take-over' ('*overname*'). The result of this is that the Code also applies to a public offer by a majority shareholder who wants to acquire the other shares. In this way the interests of minority shareholders are thought to be protected as well.

1203 The management of the offeror, as a rule, has to make contact with the management of the offeree before the public offer is announced. A public announcement then has to be made as soon as negotiations have reached a stage at which agreement may be expected. It may, however, well be that the management of the offeree is not interested in any negotiations, in which case the management of the offeror has to inform the offeree in writing of the contents of and reasons for the offer before making any public announcement.

It may also be, that disclosure of the offeror's intentions should be made public at an earlier stage, e.g. in the case of unwanted price developments of the offeree's shares on the Stock Exchange–possibly through 'leaks'–and in this case it is enough for the offeror to confirm or to deny that a take-over is contemplated. If a public offer is contemplated, no details need be given at that stage. This provision aims at ensuring that the price of the shares on the Stock Exchange develops in a 'justifiable' way and at preventing shareholders with 'inside' knowledge from taking advantage of the developments.

Prior to the public offer being announced, the SER Merger Control Committee, the Ministry of Economic Affairs and the Trade Union(s) concerned have to be informed by the offeror.

As soon as the offeror has fixed (whether or not in agreement with the offeree) the price–or where an exchange of shares is proposed: the exchange rate for the shares in the offeree–this has to be announced and details should be filed with the Committee and the Board of the Amsterdam Stock Exchange. The offeror must then prepare an 'Offering Document' which must be made available to all shareholders.

The Code indicates in detail what sort of information must be given in the Offering Document, with the aim of ensuring that the shareholders are informed to the fullest possible extent in order to enable them to decide whether they want to accept the offer.

The Code imposes a rather strict time-schedule which is mainly meant to minimise the adverse effect of 'inside' knowledge.

1204 The management of the offeree must subsequently convene an EGM at which the offer must be discussed and at which it has to disclose its views on the offer to the shareholders (unless a statement to that effect was already incorporated in the Offering Document).

The Code lays down an exhaustive list of conditions under which the offeror may withdraw his offer, but if the offeror proceeds with the offer there is a prohibition against acquiring any further shares in the offeree, on more favourable terms for the holder than the terms of the public offer, for a period of three years after the date of the public offer, unless permission of the Committee is obtained or these shares are acquired on the Stock Exchange.

1205 Chapter II deals with the protection of the interests of employees and are of a somewhat broader effect. The provisions of this chapter are applicable not only to take-overs by public offer but also in any other event which causes a change of control of the activities of a Dutch undertaking having 100 or more employees. A 'change of control' in this chapter, in general, means the transfer of 50 % or more of the company's issued shares or the transfer of a considerable part of its assets.

It should be noted that the terminology differs from that used in Chapter I in that now it speaks of '*fusies*'.

1206 The provisions, as in Chapter I, presuppose that the offerer, before making any offer, has entered into negotiations with the offeree's management. On that basis, before making an announcement (in the case of a public offer) or signing the Vending Agreement, the managements of both the offeror and the offeree have to inform the appropriate Trade Unions and must discuss with them the expected consequences of the take-over. Of particular interest in these talks are subjects relating to:

- compensation for possible disadvantageous effects of the take-over for the employees;
- the social policy after the take-over;
- the time at which the take-over is to be discussed with the Works Council pursuant to the Works Council Act (see § 705 above);
- the time at which all employees will be informed.

1207 All information given to the Trade Unions must be kept confidential for a period agreed upon by the negotiating parties and the Trade Union concerned.

If no agreement is reached between the offeror and the offeree, and the offeror nevertheless wants to proceed with the take-over, the Trade Unions must be informed by the offeror before any public announcement related to the offer is made. The management is then, as soon as practicable, given the opportunity to express its ideas and wishes to the Trade Union concerned. As soon as the decision on the take-over is made the Committee has to be informed as well, unless this had already been done at an earlier stage.

1208 Chapter III provides that in all cases where Trade Unions must be informed, the managements of all companies involved have to inform the Ministry of Economic Affairs of their negotiations.

It should be noted that the provision of Chapter III is not applicable if no negotiations between offeror and offeree take place (e.g. where the offeree refuses to co-operate).

The Ministry has the right to ask for any further information or explanations it deems desirable and in particular the Ministry should be informed of the probable economic and social consequences of the take-over. The Ministry is in this way put in a position to comment on the proposed take-over wherever that is thought appropriate.

1209 Chapter IV deals with the Merger Control Committee, its composition, its procedural rules and its powers.

The basic task of the Committee is to ensure that the provisions of the Code are observed. As already mentioned in the beginning of this review, its powers of sanction are limited to the issue of either a 'public notice' or a 'public rebuke'. Although the Code lacks the force of statutory law, the effect of such an announcement is serious enough in that the Board of the Amsterdam Stock Exchange will ask the Members of the Stockbrokers Association to discontinue their acting on behalf of the person or company that has been rebuked. Under the bye-laws of the Amsterdam Association the members have to comply with this request. The announcement may therefore result in a situation in which the offender will find it impossible to trade on the Stock Exchange or otherwise to complete any transfer of securities requiring the intermediary of an Association Member, and, therefore, e.g. will be prevented from finalising the proposed take-over.

English law

1210 Apart from S. 209 of the 1948 Act, the Companies Acts do not make any provision for take-over bids, that is an attempt by one company to acquire another otherwise than through the use of provisions of SS. 206 and 208 (see §§ 1124/5 above).

1211 However, take-over bids are regulated in a number of other ways. Firstly there is provision in the Prevention of Fraud Act (S. 14) making it a criminal offence to distribute or cause to be distributed circulars containing any invitation to persons or any information calculated to lead directly or indirectly to the doing by the recipient of various acts and, particularly for the present purpose, entering into any agreement for the acquiring or disposing of securities. This provision does not apply in various strictly defined circumstances. Of particular interest for the present purpose is the fact that it does not apply to any document the distribution of which is permitted by the Department of Trade & Industry, to the distribution of documents by or on behalf of a company to holders of its securities or to its employees or creditors, or to distribution of documents by exempted dealers, by recognised stockbrokers or by persons or bodies licensed by the Department of Trade & Industry to do so. A person or company in the last category is commonly referred to as a 'licensed dealer'. Licensed dealers are expected to comply with a set of rules (the 'licensed dealers' rules) laid down by the Department of Trade & Industry as to the methods of making offers and the contents of documents. Failure to comply is not an offence but incurs the risk of withdrawal of licence. Many merchant banks and other bodies engaged in the securities business in financial centres in the United Kingdom are exempted or licensed dealers. Exempted dealers are not bound to observe the licensed dealers' rules but they, stockbrokers, and others professionally engaged in take-over transactions, are expected to do so.

1212 In the case of listed companies, the Stock Exchange has detailed regulations for acquisitions and disposals of interests in other companies, particularly directed towards ensuring that shareholders are kept appropriately informed about such activities by their company. The extent of information depends upon the size of the transaction in relation to the company. In addition to this, the Stock Exchange requires listed companies to comply with the provisions of the City Code on Take-overs and Mergers.

The City Code on Take-overs and Mergers

1213 The introduction to the Code says that 'it represents the collective opinion of those professionally concerned in the field of take-overs and mergers on a range of business standards'. The Code is administered and enforced by the Panel on Take-overs and Mergers, which is a body representative of various institutions and professional associations in the City of London, which is, of course, the principal financial centre of the United Kingdom. The Panel has an executive body which is available for consultation, frequently by telephone, upon questions of interpretation of the Code. If necessary an appeal can be made to the full Panel which can be convened at very short notice. In the event of an apparent breach of the Code, the person alleged to be in breach is invited to be heard before the full Panel and there is a right of appeal to an appeal committee of the Panel. If a breach is found, the sanctions may be private reprimand, public censure or action designed to deprive the offender temporarily or permanently of his ability to enjoy the facilities of the securities market. In this latter connection, it should be noted that The Stock Exchange co-operates closely with the Panel and accordingly suspension of listing of a company's securities is a possibility.

The Code consists of general principles followed by more detailed rules. As the Code with associated notes on points of practice ('Practice Notes') published from time to time by the Panel is of some length, it is proposed to convey an impression of its contents by setting out the general principles in full and where appropriate adding comments to illustrate some of the ways in which they are applied in the detailed rules.

General Principle 1

1215 'It is considered to be impracticable to devise rules in such detail as to cover all the various circumstances which arise in take-over or merger transactions.

Accordingly, persons engaged in such transactions should be aware that the spirit as well as the precise wording of these General Principles and of the ensuing Rules must be observed. Moreover, it must be accepted that the General Principles and the spirit of the Code will apply in areas or circumstances not explicitly covered by any Rule'.

Comment

1216 The introduction to the Code states that it was drafted with quoted (i.e. listed) public companies particularly in mind. However, Practice Note No. 1 amplifies this and provides, inter alia, (i) that both listed and unlisted public companies are subject to the Code, (ii) that the Panel does not expect to be consulted in a merger or take-over of a private company by a public company (although it would expect the general principles to be observed and if it resulted in a change of control of a public company, the Code would apply), and (iii) that the Code applies in the case of a take-over of a public company by a private company.

General Principle 2

1217 'While the Boards of an offeror and of an offeree company and their respective advisers and associates have a primary duty to act in the best interests of their respective shareholders, they must accept that there are limitations in connection with take-over and merger transactions on the manner in which the pursuit of those interests can be carried out. Inevitably therefore these General Principles and the ensuing Rules will impinge on the freedom of action of Boards and persons involved in such transactions'.

Comment

1218 Rule 9 of the Code states that 'shareholders in companies which are effectively controlled by their directors must accept that in respect of any offer the attitude of their Board will be decisive'. It does however impose a duty on the Board to examine very closely its motives if it rejects an offer or prefers a lower offer where there is more than one offer for the company. Nevertheless, there is no obligation on directors to seek out or encourage take-over bids for their company.

General Principle 3

1219 'Shareholders shall have in their possession sufficient evidence, facts and opinions upon which an adequate judgement and decision can be reached and shall have sufficient time to make an assessment and decision. No relevant information shall be withheld from them'.

Comment

1220 Under Rule 5, when any serious intention to make an offer is received by a Board they must inform the shareholders without delay by Press notice, a copy of which should also normally be sent to each shareholder.

Under Rule 14, any document or advertisement addressed to shareholders, whether it is the offer document itself or a document supporting or recommending acceptance or rejection of an offer, must state that the directors of the relevant company have taken all reasonable care to ensure that the facts stated and opinions expressed are fair and accurate and, where appropriate, that no material factors or considerations have been omitted.

Under Rule 22, an offer must initially be open for at least twenty-one days after posting.

General Principle 4

1221 'At no time after a bona fide offer has been communicated to the Board of an offeree company or after the Board of an offeree company has reason to believe that a bona fide offer is imminent shall any action be taken by the Board of the offeree company in relation to the affairs of the company, without the approval in general meeting of the shareholders of the offeree company, which could effectively result in any bona fide offer being frustrated or in the shareholders of the offeree company being denied an opportunity to decide on its merits'.

Comment

1222 Under Rule 10, directors whose shareholdings effectively control the company, must not transfer effective control to a buyer unless the buyer undertakes to extend the same offer within a reasonable period of time to the holders of the remaining capital of the same class and a comparable offer to the holders of any other class of equity share capital or unless the Panel has agreed otherwise.

There is a corresponding obligation on the buyer under Rule 34 to make such an offer. Under Rule 38 the Board of an offeree company must not without the approval of the GM issue shares, or rights to subscribe or convert into shares, sell or acquire assets of material amount, or enter into contracts otherwise than in the ordinary course of business, once they have reason to believe a bona fide take-over is imminent. The only exceptions to this are (i) where there is an existing contractual commitment or (ii) the Panel gives its consent in special circumstances. Among other things, this Rule excludes the practice–at present very much '*en vogue*' in the Netherlands–which formerly took place as a defence to an unwelcome take-over bid, of issuing new shares to a 'friend' so as to prevent the unwelcome bidder gaining control.

General Principle 5

1223 'It must be the object of all parties to a take-over or merger transaction to use every endeavour to prevent the creation of a false market in the shares of an offeror or offeree company'.

Comment

1224 Apart from the obligation as to prompt announcement referred to above, under Rule 30 no dealings of any kind in the shares of the offeree company by any person or company, other than the offeror, who knows of the preliminary discussion, may take place between the time when there is reason to suppose that an approach is contemplated and announcement of it. Similarly if the price of an offeror company's shares would be sensitive to the proposed offer, no dealing must take place in those either.

General Principle 6

1225 'A Board which receives an offer, or is approached with a view to an offer being made, should normally in the interests of its shareholders seek competent outside advice'.

No comment.

General Principle 7

1226 'Rights of control must be exercised in good faith and the oppression of a minority is wholly unacceptable'.

No comment.

General Principles 8 and 9

1227 'All shareholders of the same class of an offeree company shall be treated similarly by an offeror'.

'If, after a take-over or merger transaction is reasonably in contemplation, an offer has been made to one or more shareholders of an offeree company, any subsequent general offer made by or on behalf of the same offeror or his associates to the shareholders of the same class shall not be on less favourable terms'.

Comment
1228 Generally offers for less than the whole of the equity share capital are considered undesirable. However under Rule 27 if the Panel gives consent to an offer for less than 100%, then it must be made to all shareholders so that they can if they wish accept in full for the relevant percentage of their holdings. Under Rule 35, a person who acquires shares carrying 40% of the voting rights of a company must, unless otherwise permitted by the Panel, make an unconditional offer to the holders of the remaining equity share capital. The offer must either be in cash or accompanied by a cash alternative at no less than the highest price paid by such person for shares of that class within the preceding twelve months. Furthermore, under Rule 33 in the case of any offer (unless the Panel permits otherwise), an offeror who with persons acting in concert with him has within the previous twelve months purchased over 15% of a class of share capital for cash, must make a cash offer or provide a cash alternative at not less than the highest price paid during that period, and under Rule 36 no offeror or person acting in concert with an offeror may enter into arrangements to deal in or purchase or sell shares of the offeree company if the arrangements involve specially favourable conditions which cannot be extended to all shareholders.

General Principle 10

1229 'During the course of a take-over or merger transaction, or when such is in contemplation, neither the offeror, the offeree company nor any of their respective advisers shall furnish information to some shareholders which is not made available to all shareholders. This principle shall not apply to the furnishing of information in confidence by an offeree company to a bona fide potential offeror or vice versa, nor to the issue of circulars by members of a Stock Exchange (who are associates of any party to the transaction) to their own investment clients provided such issue shall previously have been approved by the Panel'.

Comment
1230 Under Rule 12 any information given to a preferred bidder should on request be furnished equally and as promptly to a less welcome but bona fide potential bidder.

General Principle 11

1231 Directors of an offeror or an offeree company shall always, in advising their shareholders, act only in their capacity as Directors and not have regard to their personal or family shareholdings or their personal relationships with the companies. It is the shareholders' interests taken as a whole which should be considered, together with those of employees and creditors.

Comment

1232 Under Rule 15 an offer document should contain information about the offeror and its intentions in regard to the future of the offeree company.

General Principle 12

1233 'Any document or advertisement addressed to shareholders containing information, opinions or recommendations from the Board of an offeror or offeree compane or its respective advisers shall be treated with the same standards of care as if it were a prospectus within the meaning of the Companies Act 1948. Especial care shall by taken over profit forecasts'.

Comment

1234 Under Rule 16 the accounting basis and calculations for the forecasts must be examined and reported on by the auditors or consultant accountants and any revaluations of assets must be supported by the opinion of a named independent professional expert whose basis of valuation must be stated.

It should be noted that there is no requirement under the Companies Act, the Stock Exchange Regulations, or the Code for employees or trade unions to be consulted at any stage of a take-over or merger transaction.

Comparison

1235 The Netherlands and the United Kingdom are believed to be the only two countries in the EEC which have a code, albeit non-statutory, regarding take-over and mergers.

The draft Third EEC Directive proposes that the Member States should have *legally binding* rules in this area. The draft Directive sets out in some detail rules for the protection of shareholders, employees and creditors. These rules relate to both the acquisition of a company by another company–either for cash or in exchange for shares–and merger by formation of a new company.

1236 The Dutch Take-over Code contains three matters which are dealt with only slightly or not at all in the UK Code.

In the first place the Dutch Code, but not the UK Code, positively requires consultation with employees. Secondly, there is an obligation to keep the Government informed. This is not so in England unless there is a potential situation within the scope of the 'monopolies' legislation ('*The Fair Trading Act, 1973*'). Thirdly, there is the restriction, for three years after the take-over, on buying shares at a higher price, except on the Stock Exchange.

It should, however, be remembered that in England the provisions of the Prevention of Frauds Act (see on § 1211 above) would apply to approaches to shareholders even after completion of a take-over bid and, therefore, apart from purchases on the Stock Exchange details would have to be given of previous prices paid for the shares, although there is no absolute prohibition on purchasing at a higher price.

1237 On the other hand, the UK Take-over Code has rules obliging a purchaser of 40% of the capital of a company (or even less if effective control can be exercised without as much as 40%) to make an offer for the remaining capital. This is in contrast with the Dutch Code which does not, at least expressly, prevent a person from gaining control of a company and leaving the other shareholders 'locked in'. In Dutch literature, however, it is often contended that the acquisition of control through an 'undetected' take-over is contrary to the spirit of the Code, because in this way all safeguards laid down in the Code–especially those for the benefit of the employees–are foregone.

1238 Another protection under the UK Code which does not appear in the Dutch Code is the '15% requirement', under which an offeror has to provide cash (and not just shares or other 'paper') when he has within the previous 12 months bought over 15% of the share capital for cash.

1239 Finally it should be noted that there is no equivalent under Dutch law of the English S. 209 procedure (in the 1948 Act). Subject to some additional requirements where an offeror already holds some shares, this section enables an offeror *which is itself a company* and which has received acceptances in respect of at least 90% of the shares for which the offer was made compulsorily to acquire the remainder on the same terms and make the company concerned a wholly-owned subsidiary. This is of great utility to an offeror since it removes the problem of keeping minority shareholders contented, but without enabling them to hold the offeror up to ransom over the price of their shares.

1240 As a last point of comparison it should be stated that both Codes aim at curbing 'insider' dealings. Dutch company law does at present contain no provision in that respect, and English law is thought to have made a reference to this phenomenon only in S. 172 of the 1948 Act and S. 32 of the 1967 Act, where dealing with investigations by the Department of Trade & Industry into dealings in shares or debentures by directors or others (see in § 909 above).

A curb on 'insider dealing' in the Dutch Code is laid down in Article 8 which requires that each director and each 'Commissaris' of both the offeror and the offeree must disclose, at the moment of the public announcement, to the Merger Control Committee all information relating to their dealings–directly or indirectly–in shares or Depositary Receipts in the offeree during a period of six months preceding the first public disclosure of the take-over price or rate of exchange.

1241 Rule 17 of the English Code contains a similar provision (but covering 12 months). Despite the rules laid down in the Code there remains much concern in the United Kingdom at present about the making of unfair profits by share dealing by persons improperly using confidential information which has not been made public. So far there does not appear to be any general and effective legal remedy although The

Stock Exchange and the Take-over Panel attempt to impose some measures of control and many merchant banks and broking houses have their own internal rules.

In the White Paper the Government expresses its conclusion that in principle inside dealings should be made the subject of a criminal offence with the object of ensuring 'that anyone who is in possession of information which would be likely, if generally known, to have a material effect on the price of the relevant securities refrains from dealing until the material information has properly been made generally available'.

The White Paper recognises that there are considerable problems involved, firstly in defining who is an 'insider' and secondly whether the offence should consist of dealing *with the guilty intent* of profiting from inside information or merely of dealing *when at the same time being in possession* of price-sensitive inside information. The Government takes the view that insiders should include 'directors, employees, major shareholders and professional advisers of the company, together with the near relation- of each of these people' and that dealing when in possession of price-sensitive infors mation should be a criminal offence unless the insider 'can show that his primary intention in dealing at that particular time was not to make a profit or avoid a loss'.

The Government further considers that, on the question of civil liability, a person who profits unfairly over another by misusing materially significant information should be liable to the other person if he has suffered an identifiable loss and also that an insider should be accountable to the company for his profit.

Geschriften van de Nederlandse Vereniging voor Rechtsvergelijking

1. Prof. mr. J. G. Sauveplanne, De bescherming van de derde verkrijger te goeder trouw van roerende lichamelijke zaken.

2. Verslag van de bespreking van no. 1.

3. Prof. mr. F. H. van der Burg, Toezeggingen en pseudowetgeving in het administratieve recht; en
prof. mr. Ch. P. A. Geppaart, De rechtswaarde van niet op de wet steunende bestuurshandelingen van de belastingadministratie.

3.bis Verslag van de bespreking van no. 3.

4. Mr. J. D. van der Meulen, De belediging van hoofden van bevriende staten.

5. Prof. mr. F. J. W. Löwensteyn, De vennootschap met beperkte aansprakelijkheid.

6. Mr. L. Prakke, Toetsingsrecht.

7 Prof. dr. Z. Szirmai, De bruikbaarheid van het Sowjet burgerlijk recht voor de westerse rechtsvergelijker.

8. Prof. dr. I. Kisch, De rechtsfamilies en haar dynamiek, benevens een Verslag van de bespreking van de nummers 6 en 7.

9. Mr. W. E. Haak, De beroepsvoetballer.

10. Prof. mr. H. U. Jessurun d'Oliveira, De meerwaarde van rechterlijke uitspraken.

11. Prof. mr. H. J. M. Jeukens, Rechtsvergelijking in de jurisprudentie van het Hof van Justitie van de Europese Gemeenschappen.

12. M. G. Chester Ll.B. en mr. F. O. W. Vogelaar, English/Dutch Company Law, a comparative review.

13. Mr. A. H. J. Swart, Politiek Delikt en Asiel.

Kluwer · Deventer · Postbus 23

GPSR Compliance

The European Union's (EU) General Product Safety Regulation (GPSR) is a set of rules that requires consumer products to be safe and our obligations to ensure this.

If you have any concerns about our products, you can contact us on ProductSafety@springernature.com

In case Publisher is established outside the EU, the EU authorized representative is:

Springer Nature Customer Service Center GmbH
Europaplatz 3
69115 Heidelberg, Germany

Batch number: 10854269

Printed by Printforce, the Netherlands